JUST JESTERS
COLORING BOOK

FOR GROWN-UPS
(AND WANNABEs)

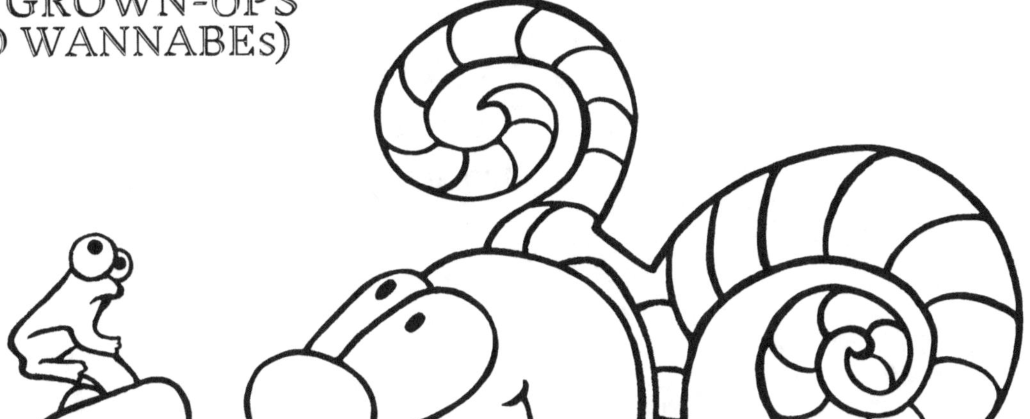

ARGYLE IMP

With love to Able.

The coloring pages in this book are all new and original art.

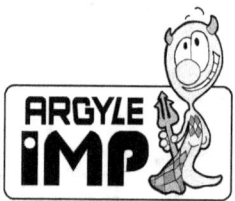

Copyright ©2018 by Argyle Imp
All rights reserved.
www.argyleimp.com

ISBN-13: 978-1-73249-950-8
ISBN-10: 1-73249-950-0

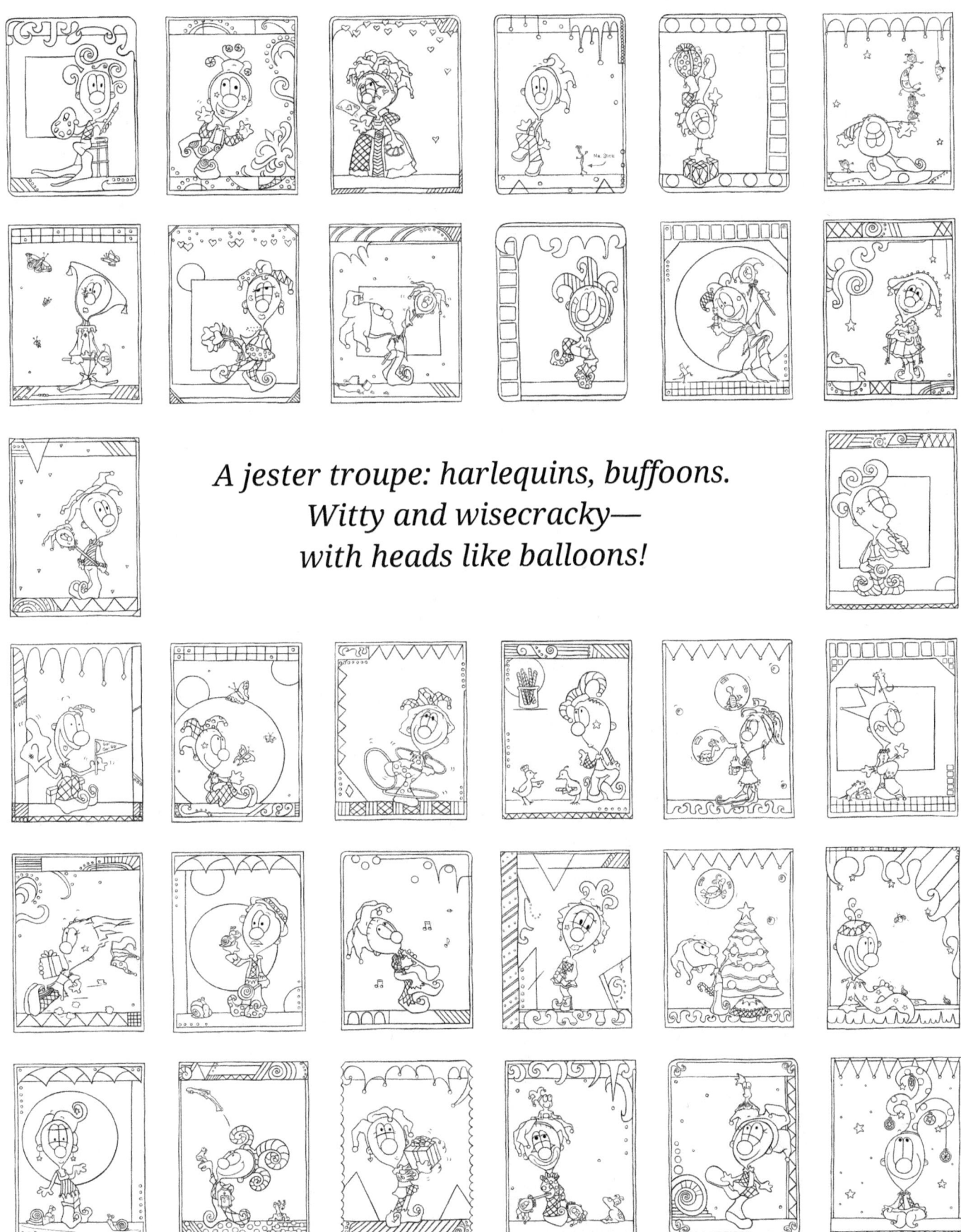

*A jester troupe: harlequins, buffoons.
Witty and wisecracky—
with heads like balloons!*

Artist is as artist does.
Color the fool...
...*just because!*

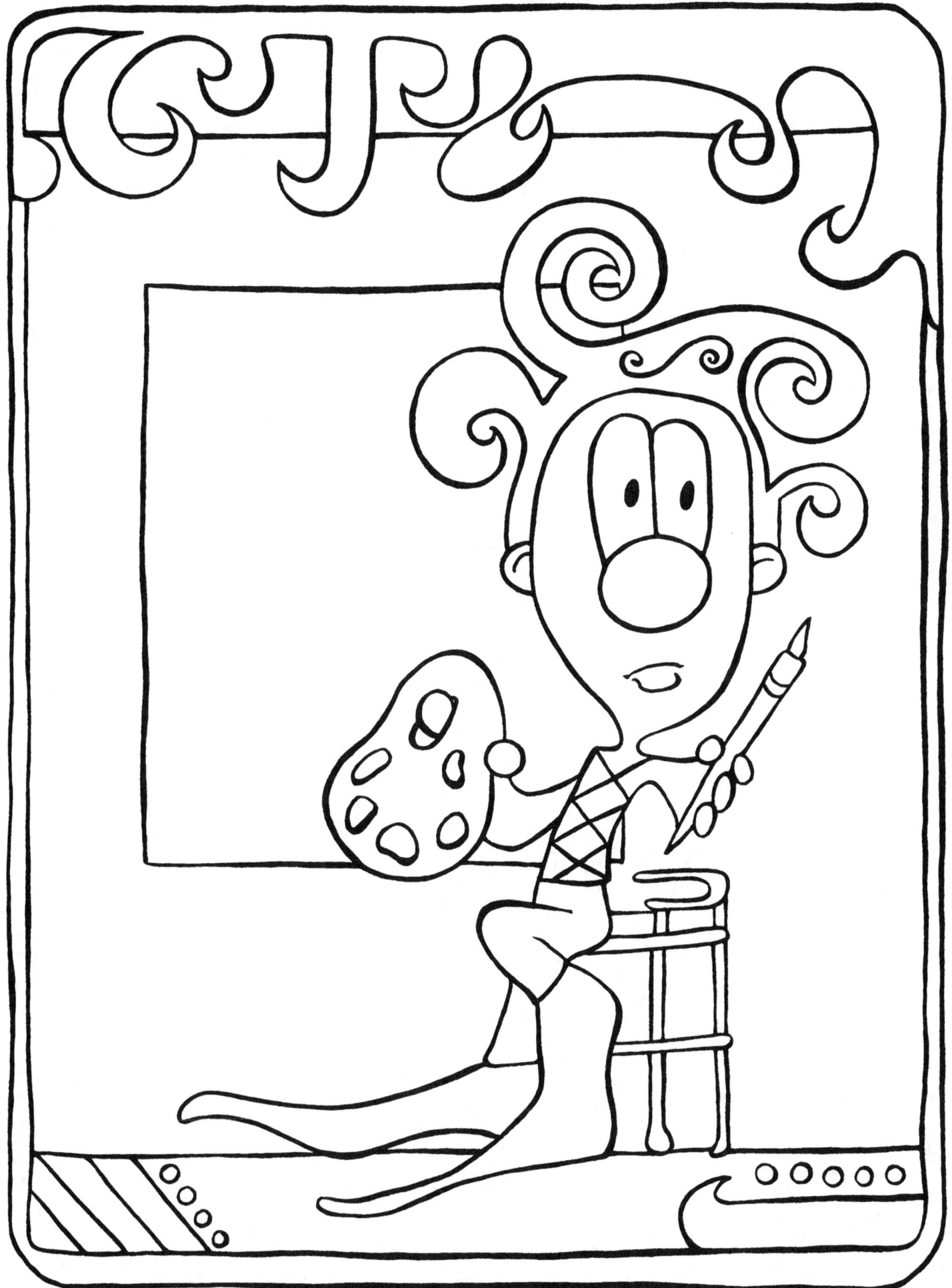

Jiggle-dee-dumb—
Wiggle-dee-dee—
Where 'er I go,
I'll always be *me*.

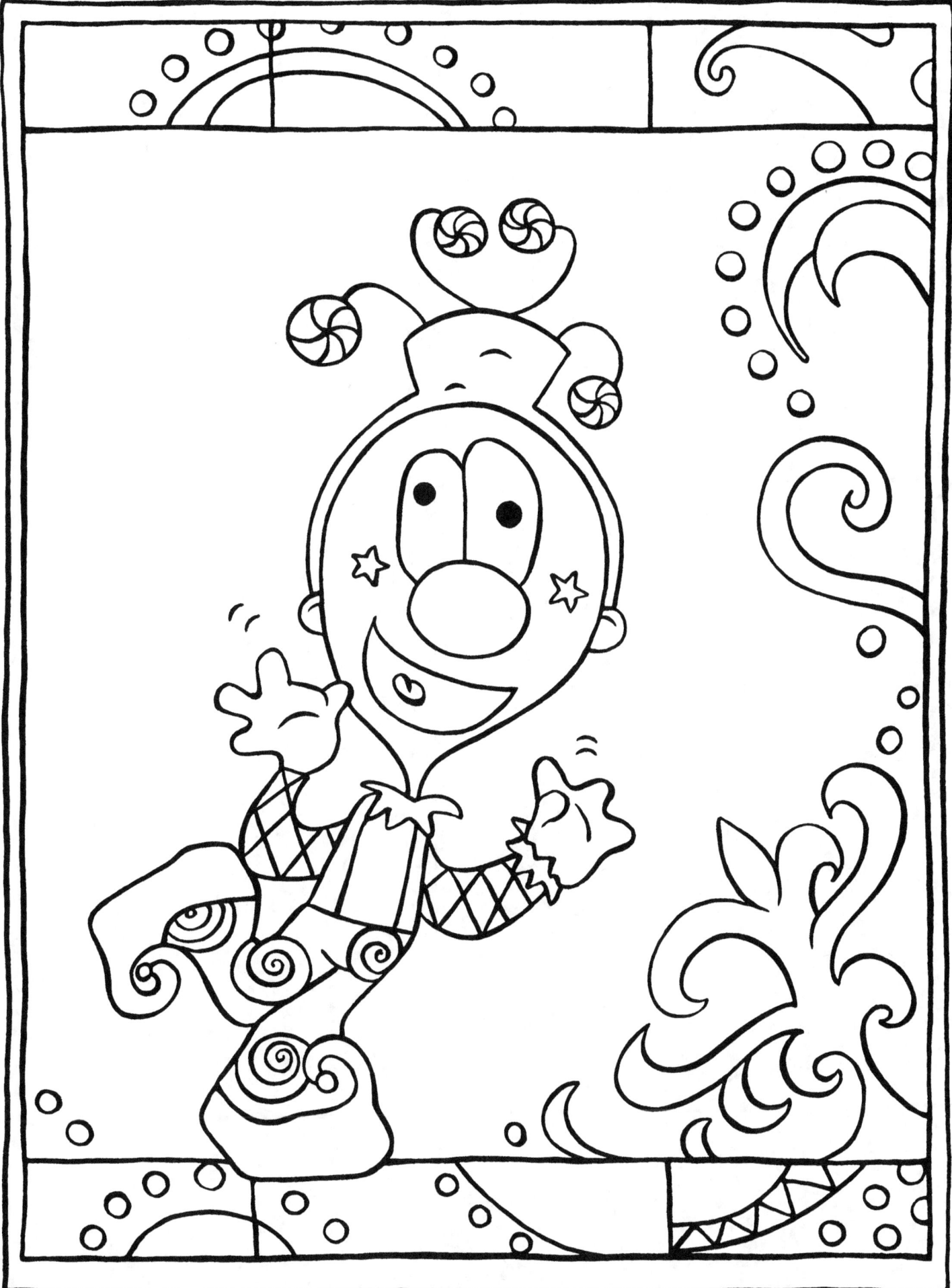

What intrigue?
In spite of everything, I have
an ace up my sleeve.

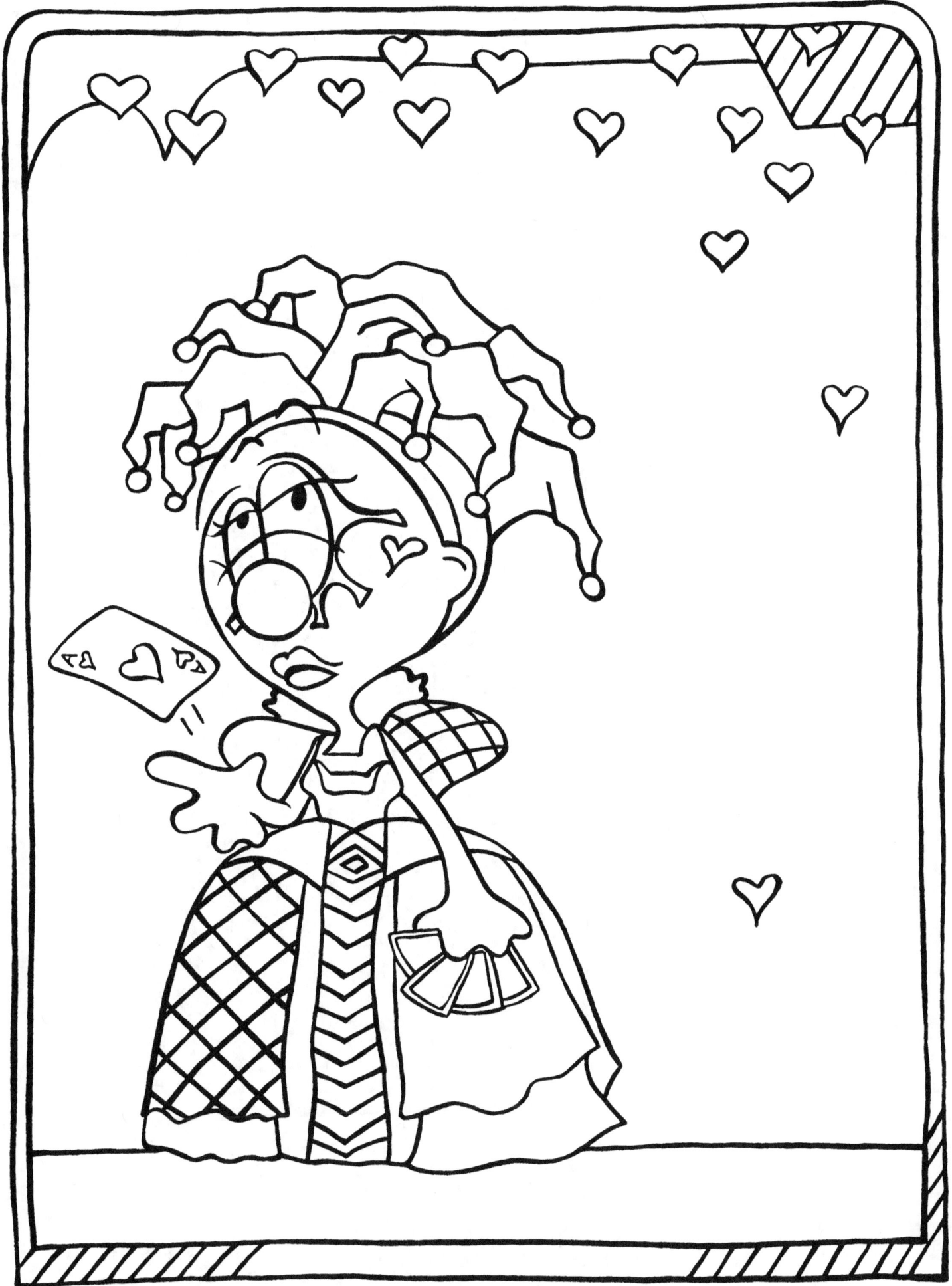

Say *Hello* to my little friend.
A little stick that speaks softly,
and laughs boldly.

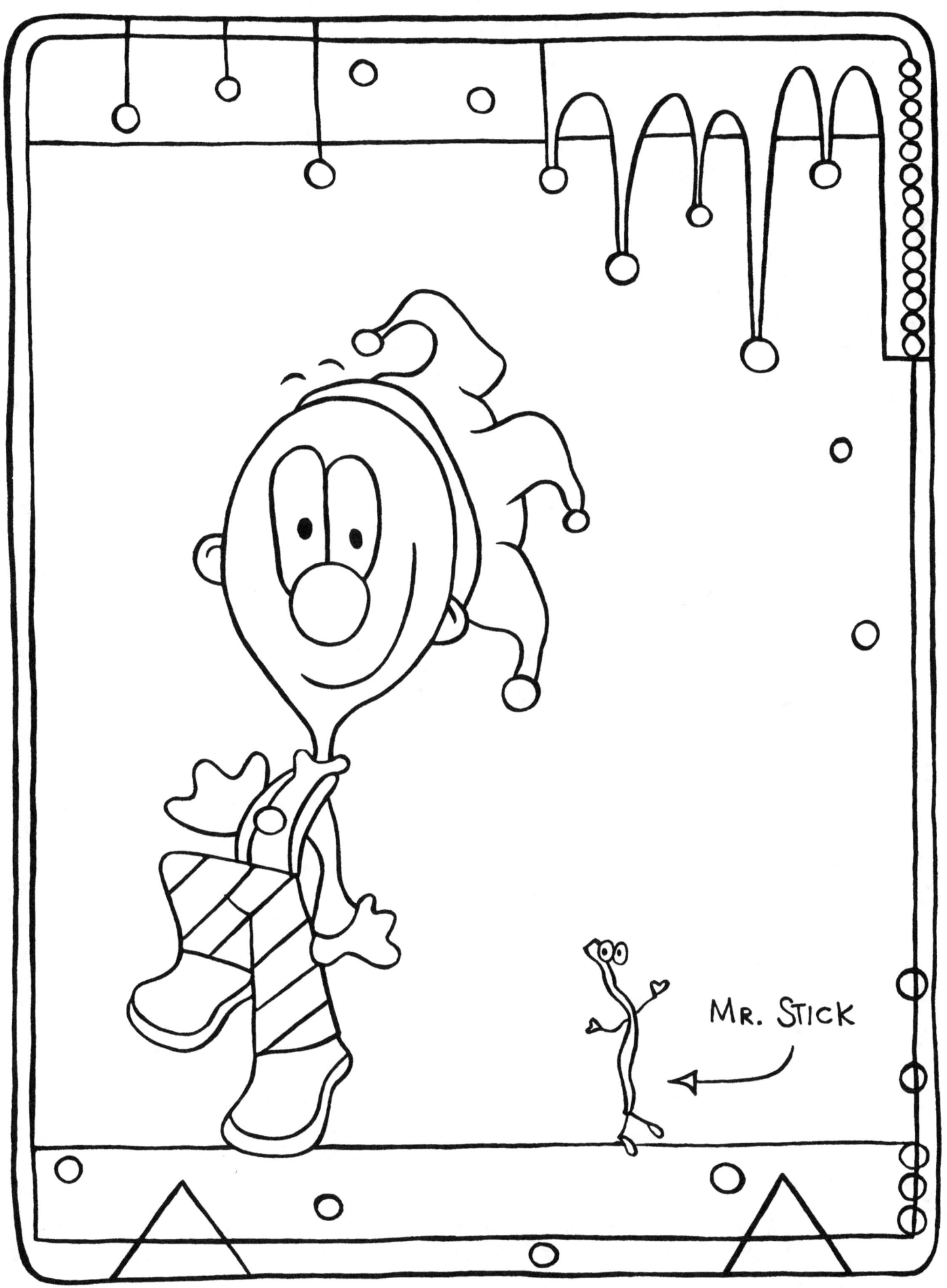

I'm so crazy I make the impossible look merely difficult, and the improbable look friggin' easy.

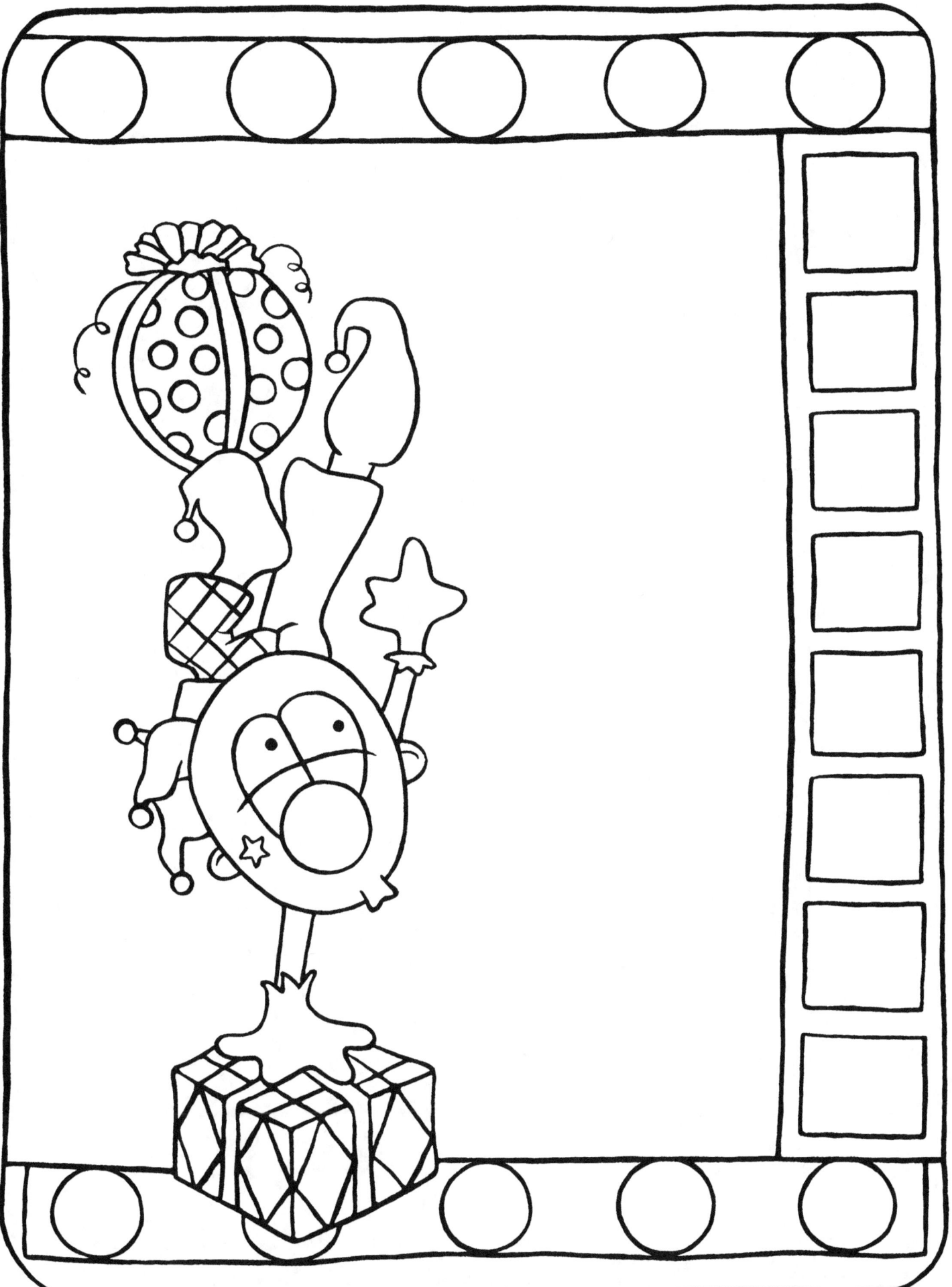

Everyone needs a resident jester.
Even when they think they don't.

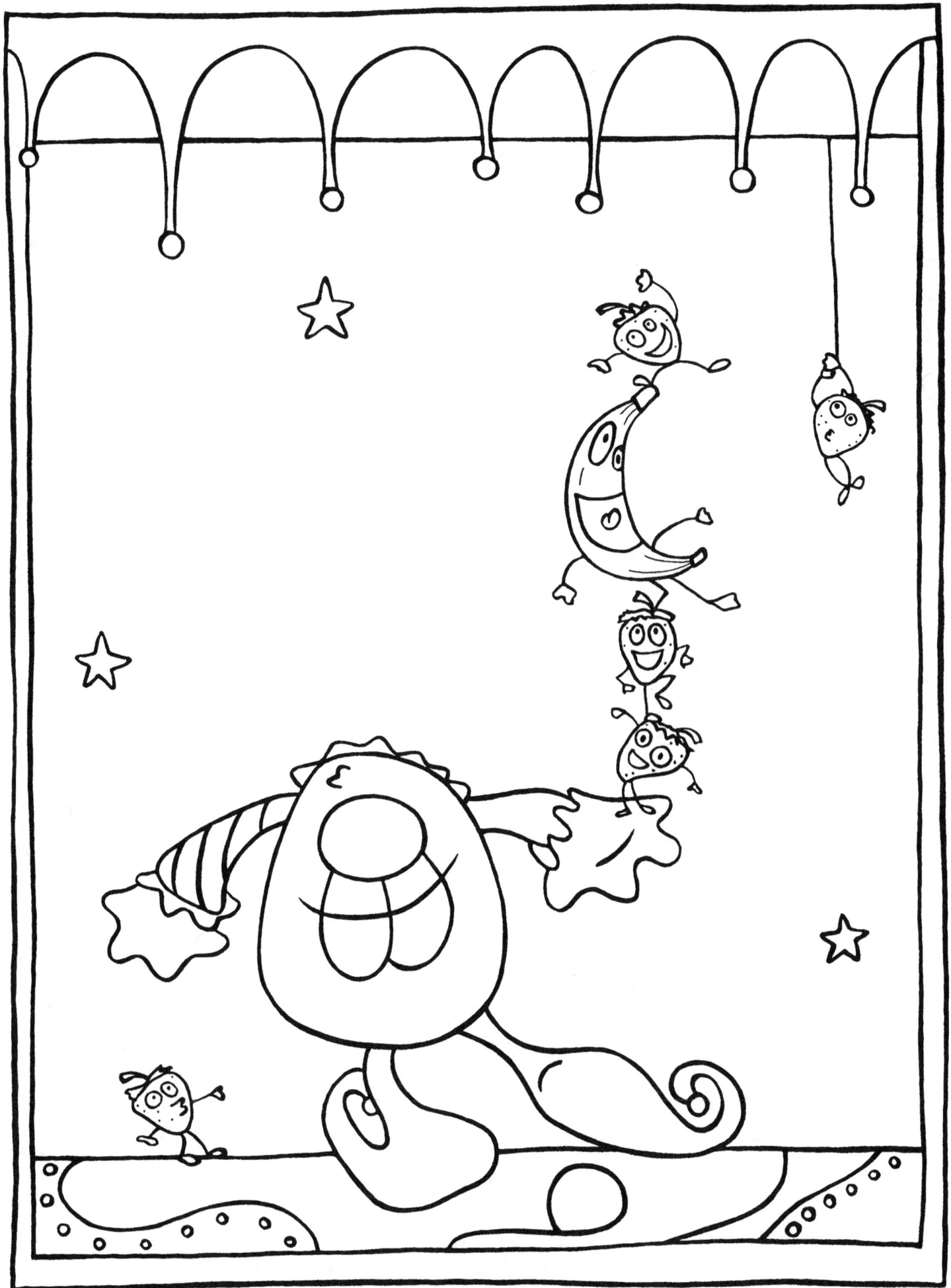

I am a mere rest stop
in butterfly migration.

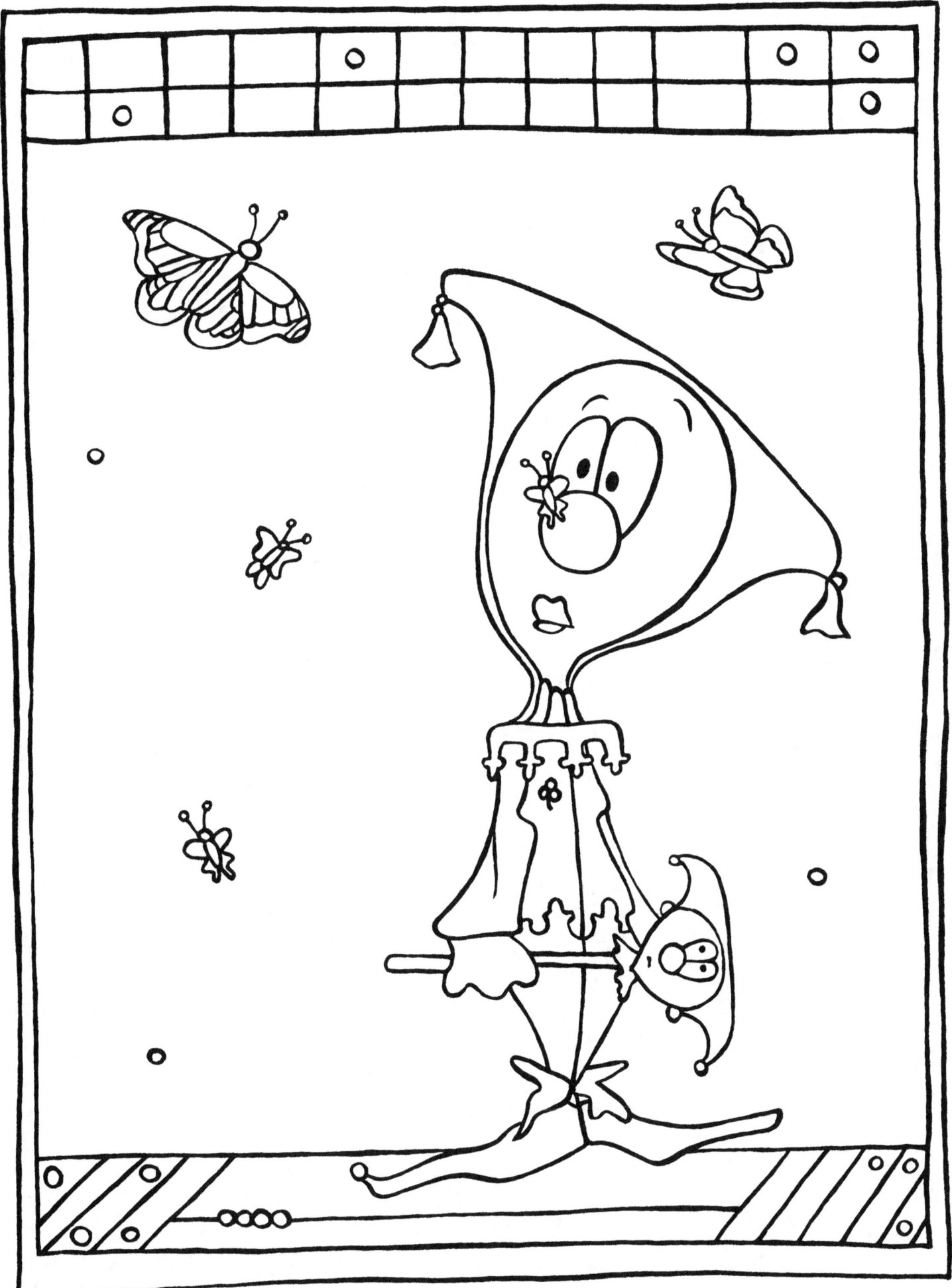

The subtle, sweet dance of
seduction begins.
You have been warned.

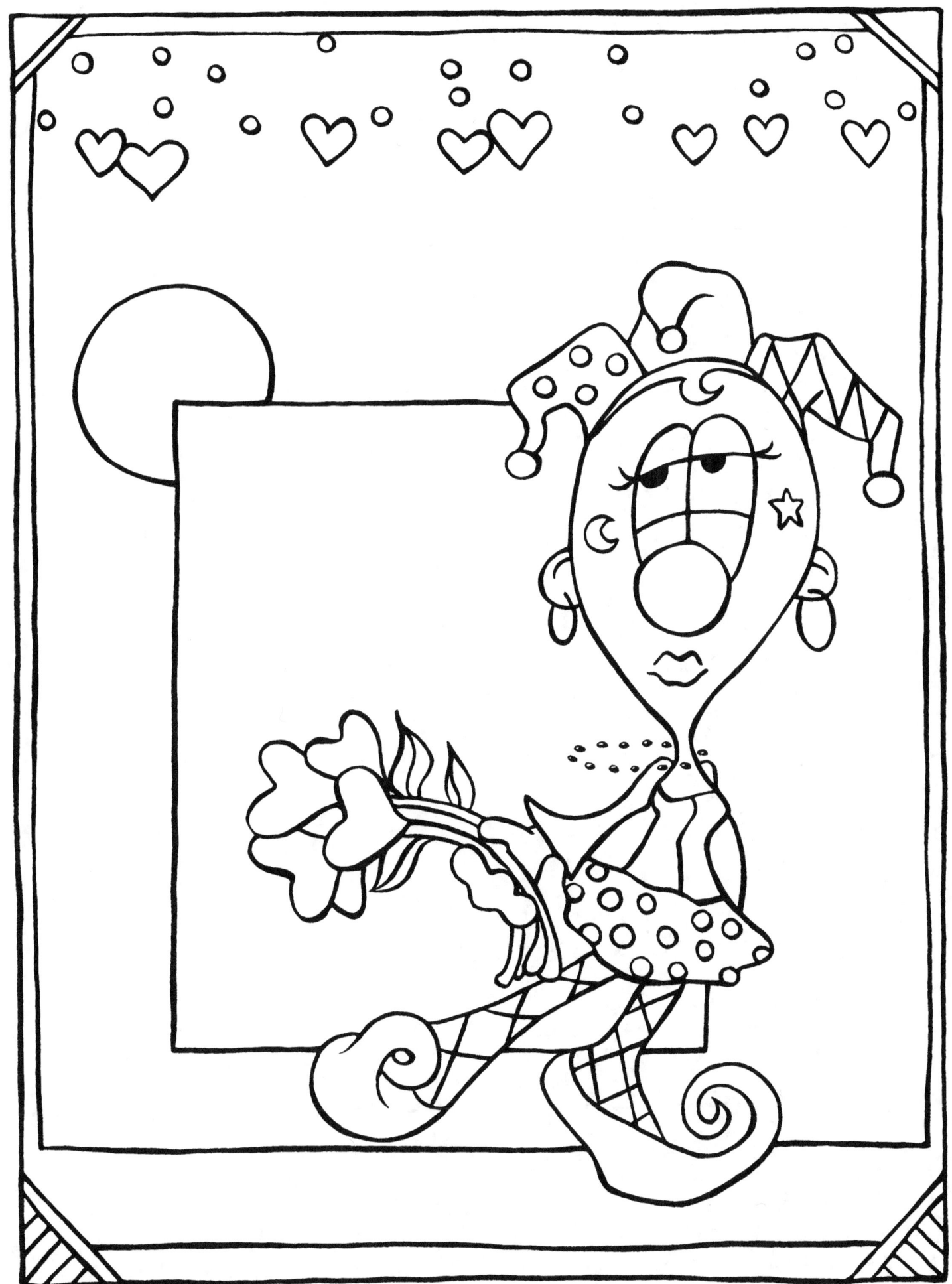

Sure. Blame the puppet—
when you're guilty as Punch.

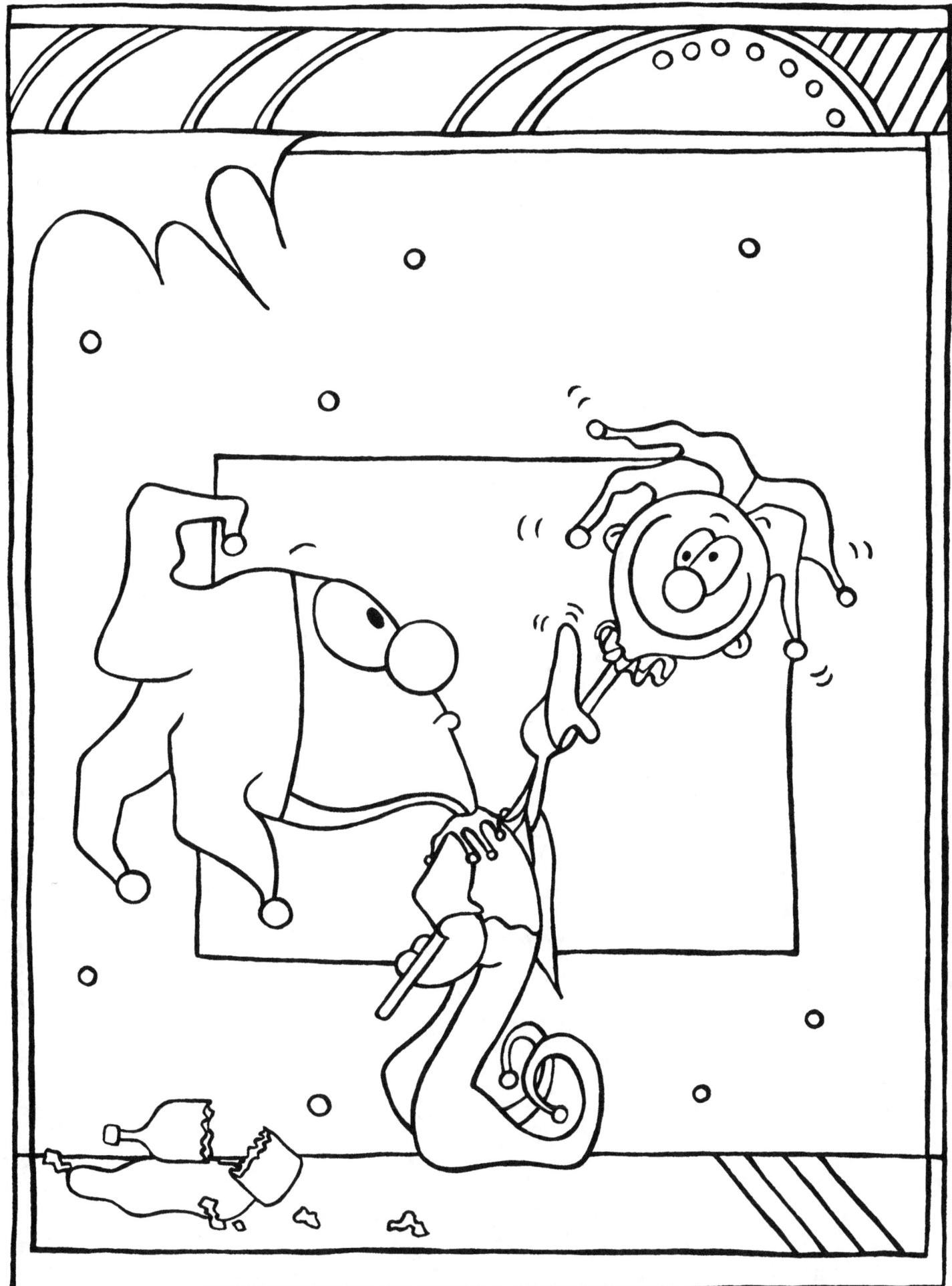

Friendship isn't about finding sane.
It's about matching crazy.

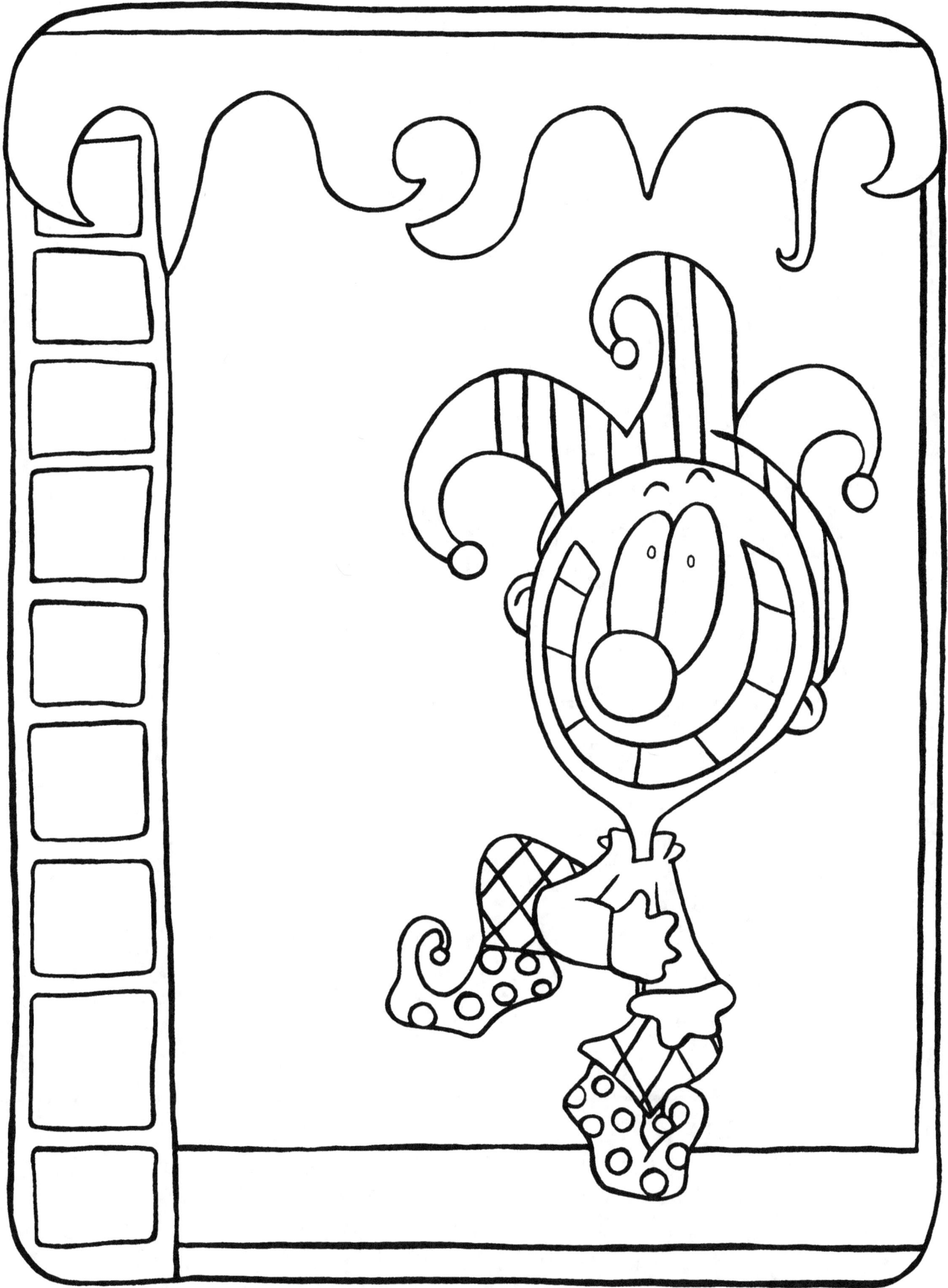

Here's to that tale of Hamelin rats,
wherein a billion gazillion
of 'em were lured to their deaths.

In our version we'll pretend they're
going to the spa for manicures.

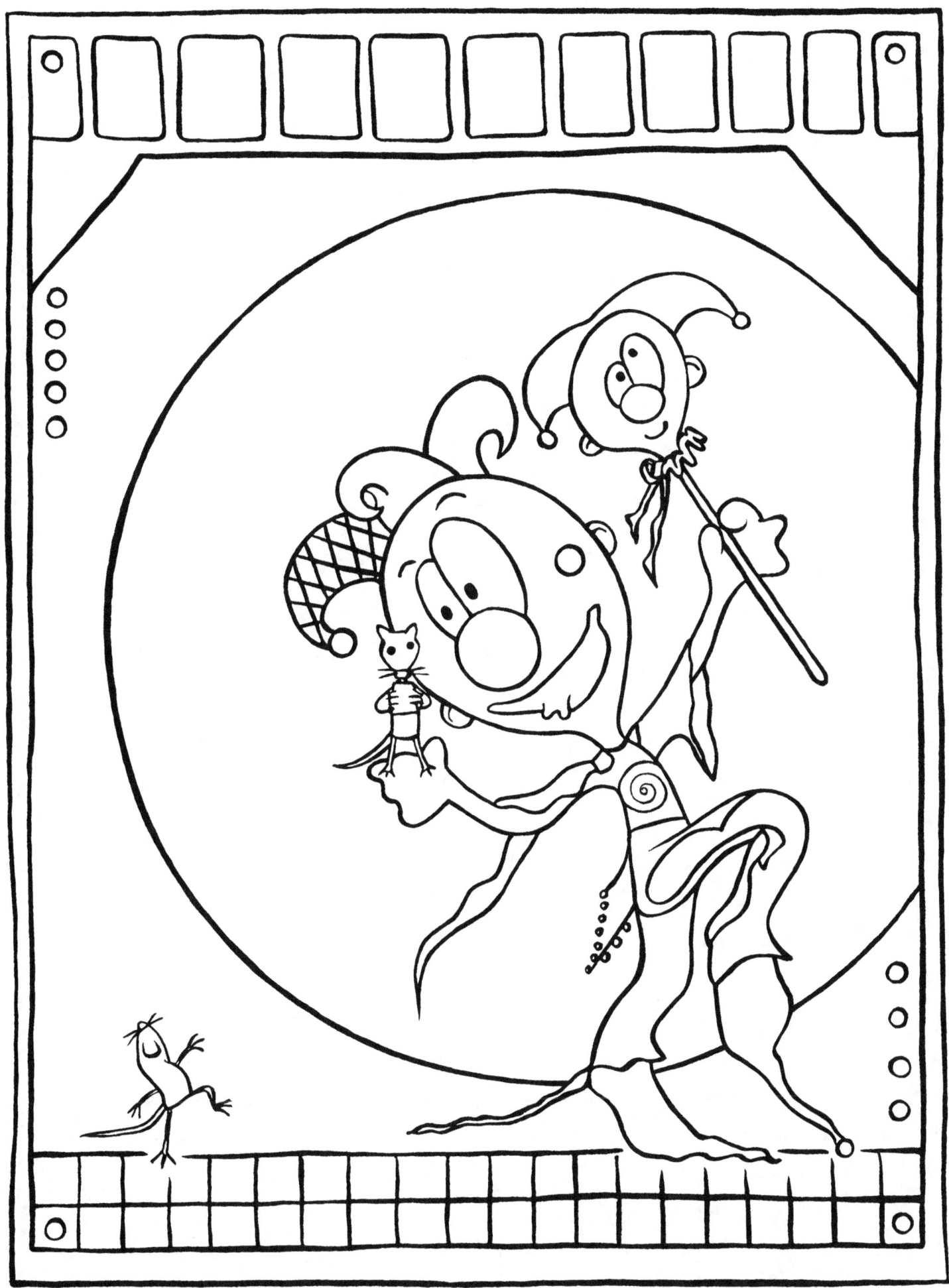

Nothing breaks round-table tensions
like the purr-power of the kitty friend.

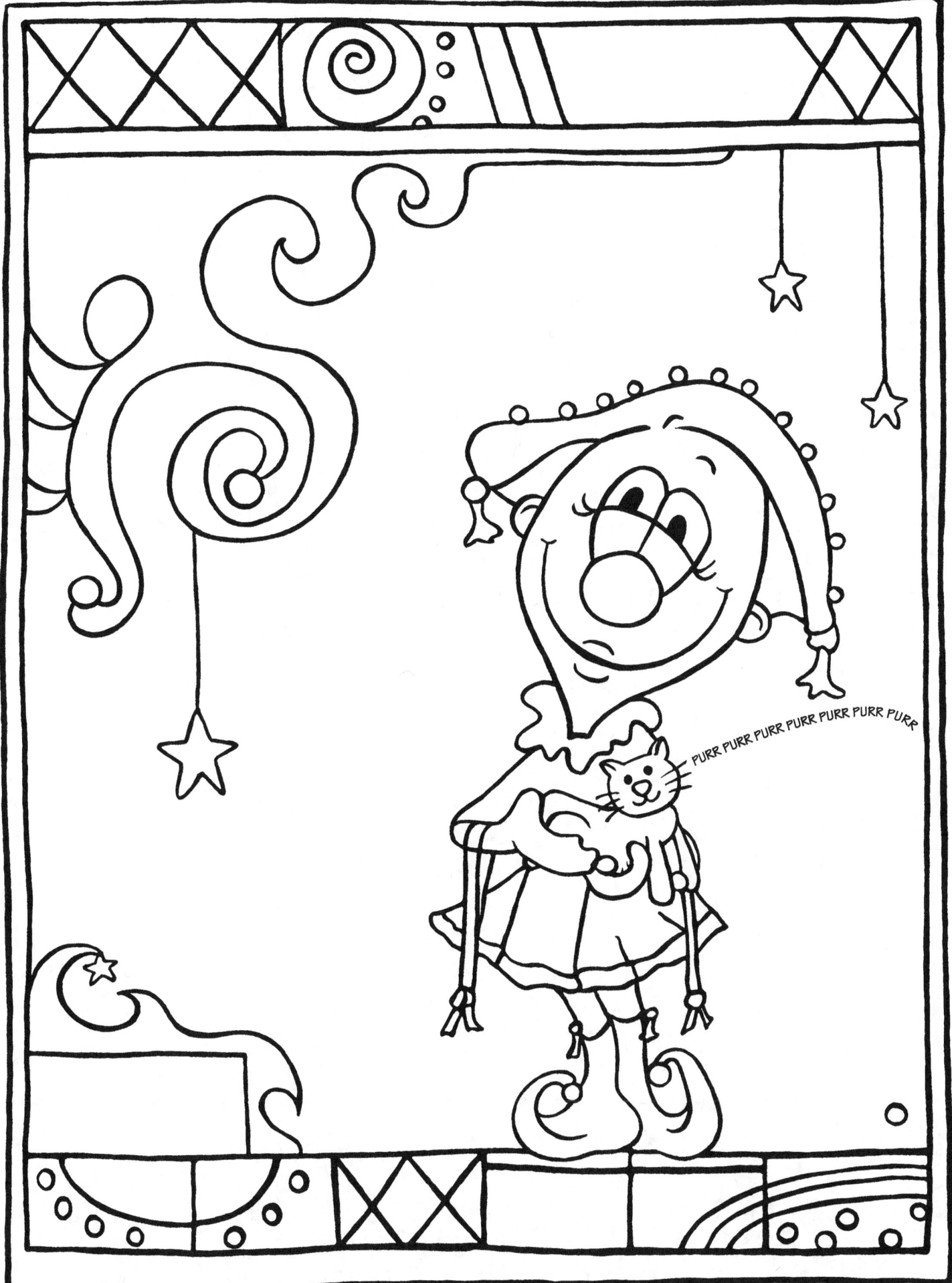

There's a flibbertigibbet somewhere about.
Or is it just whispering winds of gossip
stirring up doubt?

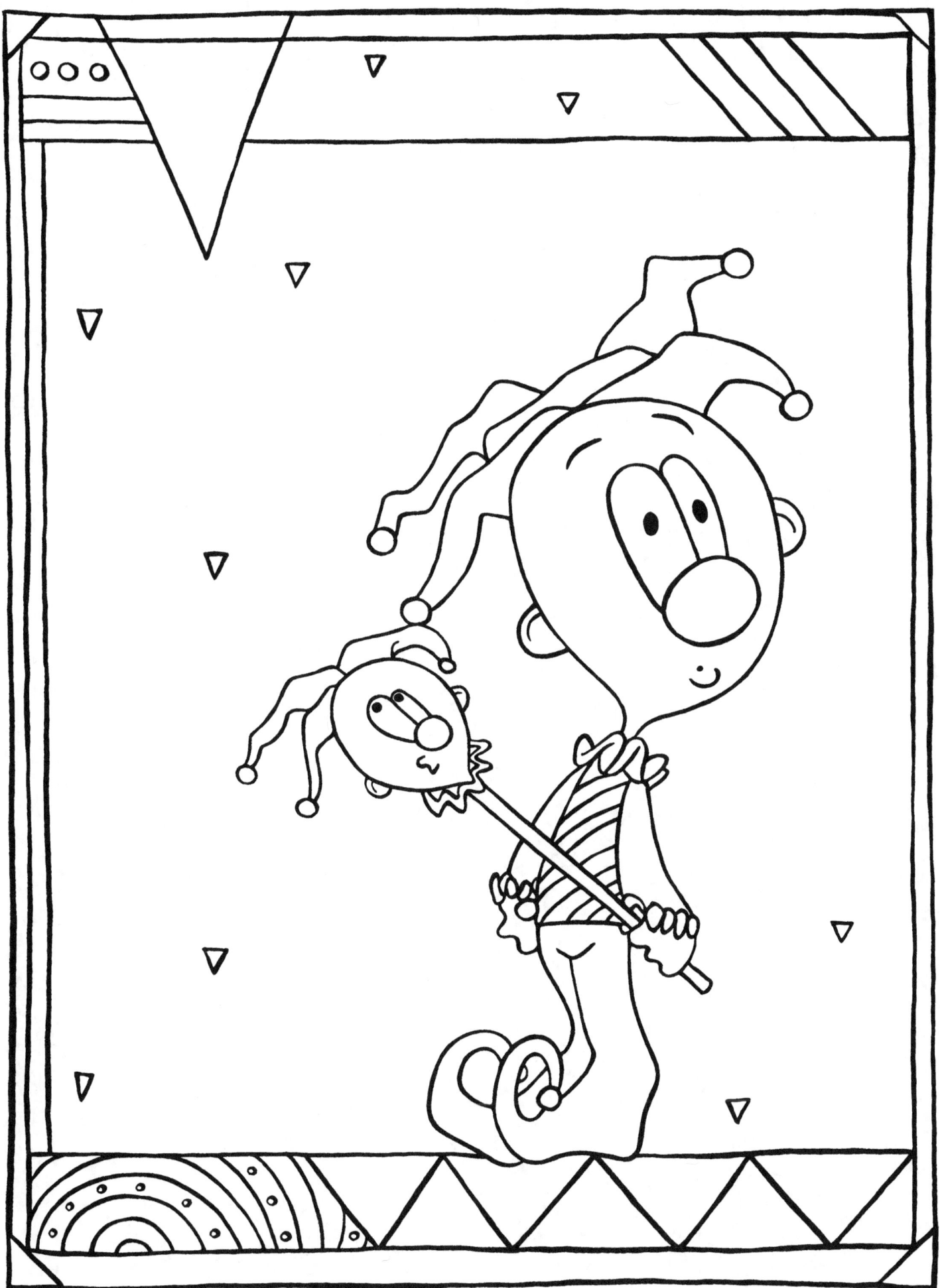

Since you're not here, and I'm all alone,
I'm gonna suck every last drop of pleasure
out of this peppermint stick.
And the lollipop, too.
Don't you wish you had one?

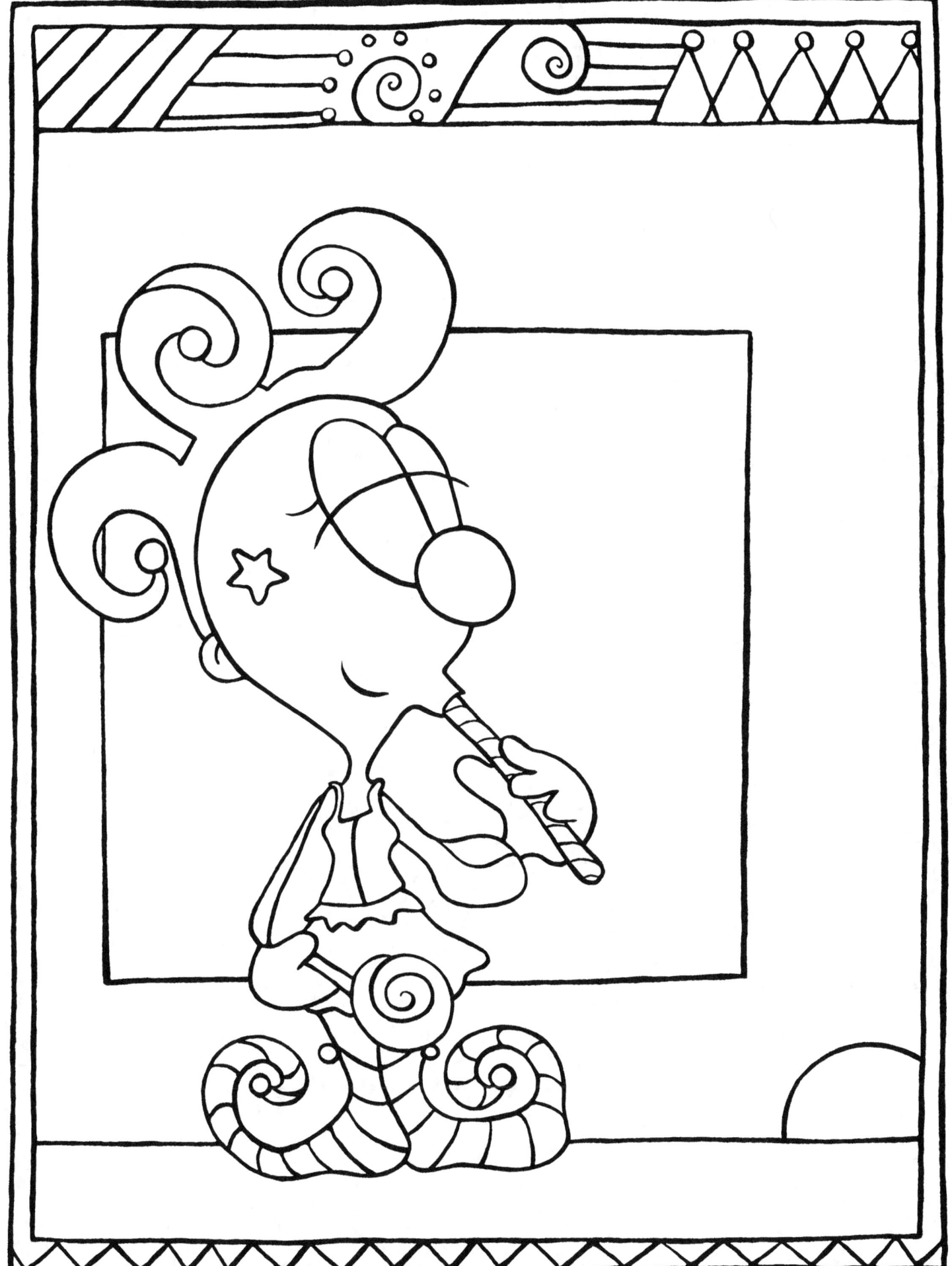

While all the brave knights
Get skewered at the tourney—
I'll joke and jab,
And lampoon their journey.

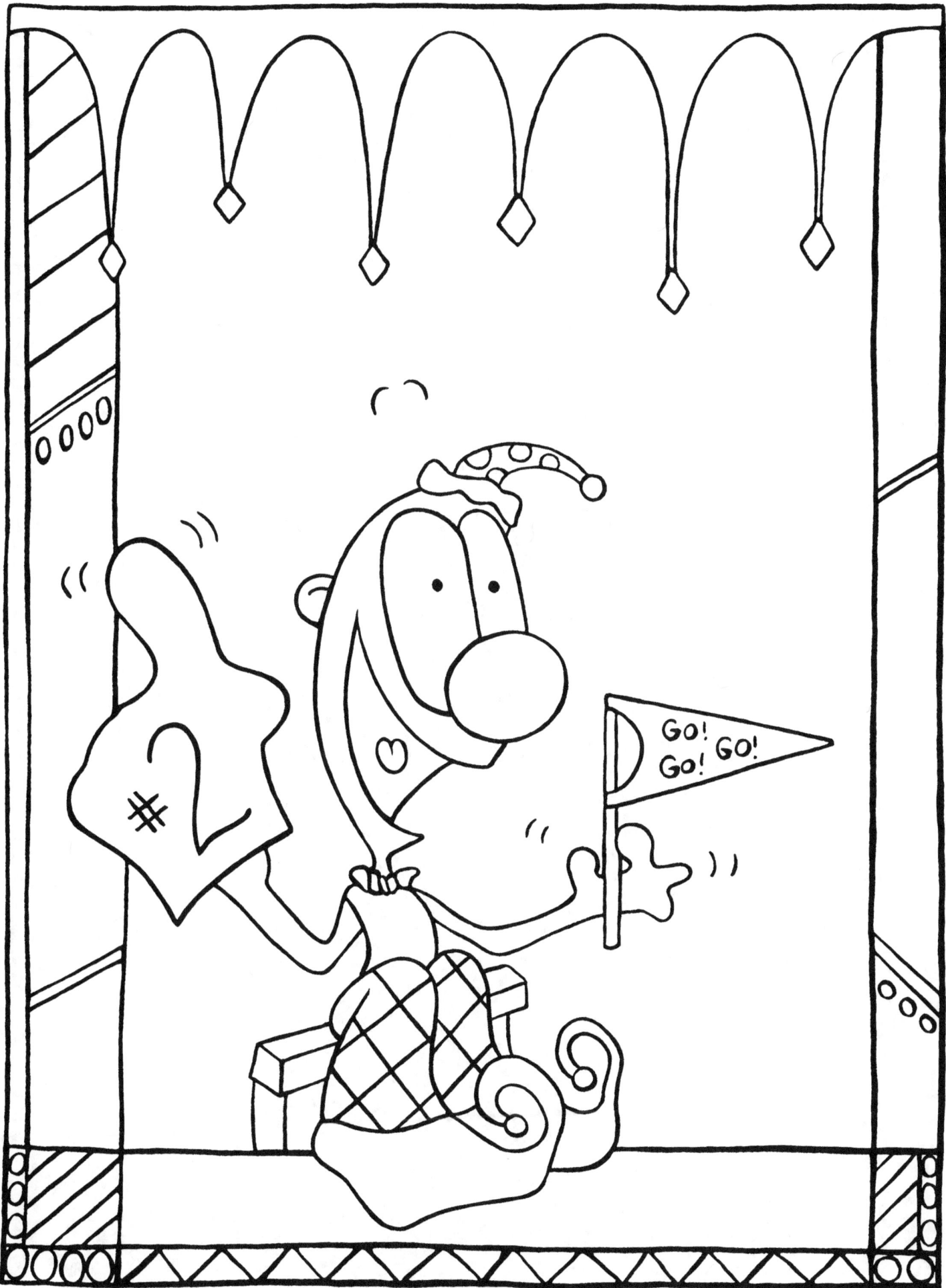

SONNET TO A BUTTERFLY
I embrace
Summer's Hot—
Just to feel the Sky
On my Skin
Like your Wings do.

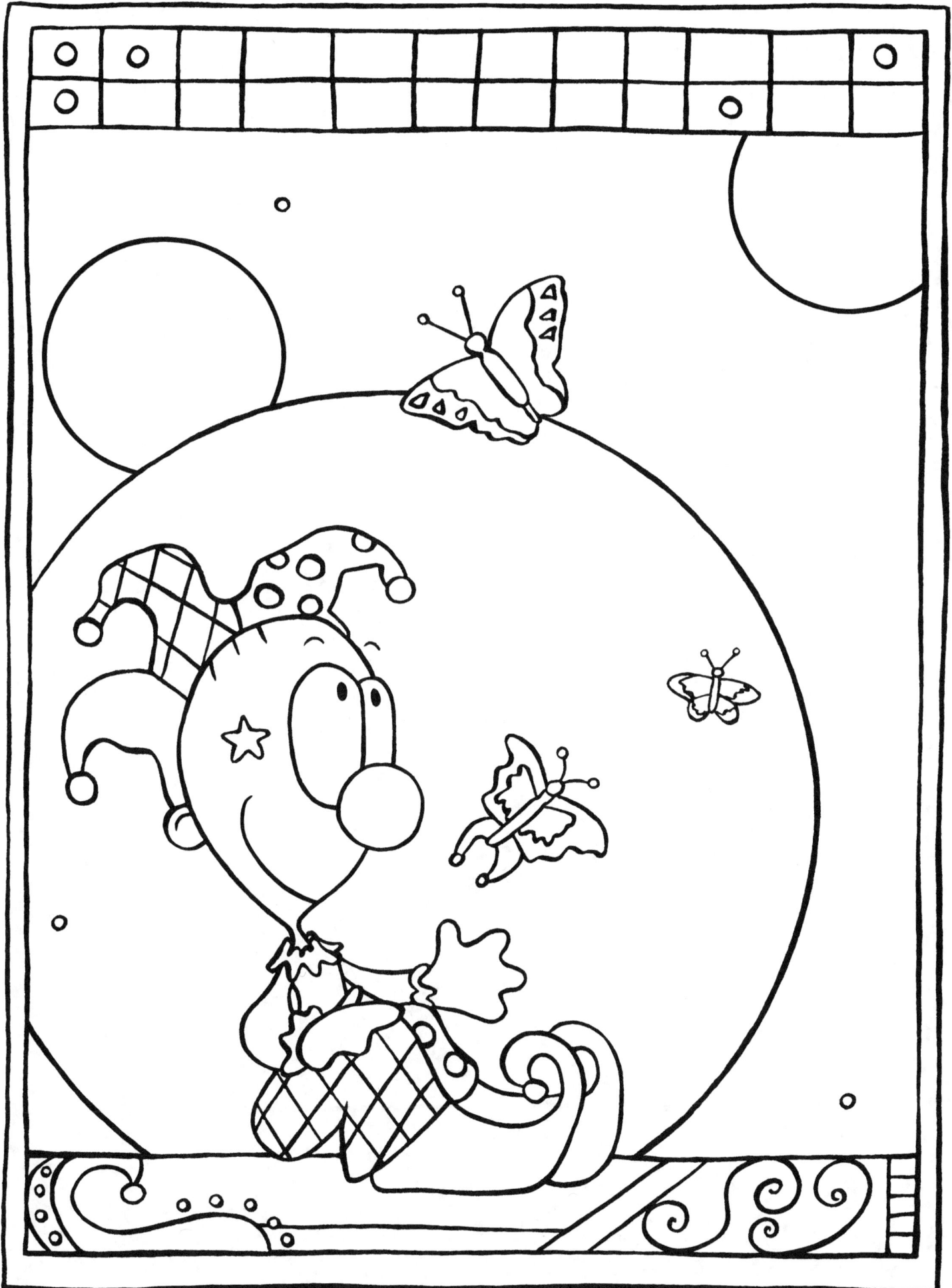

I'll not wander my life
Trying to please thee—
I'd lose myself
And never find me.

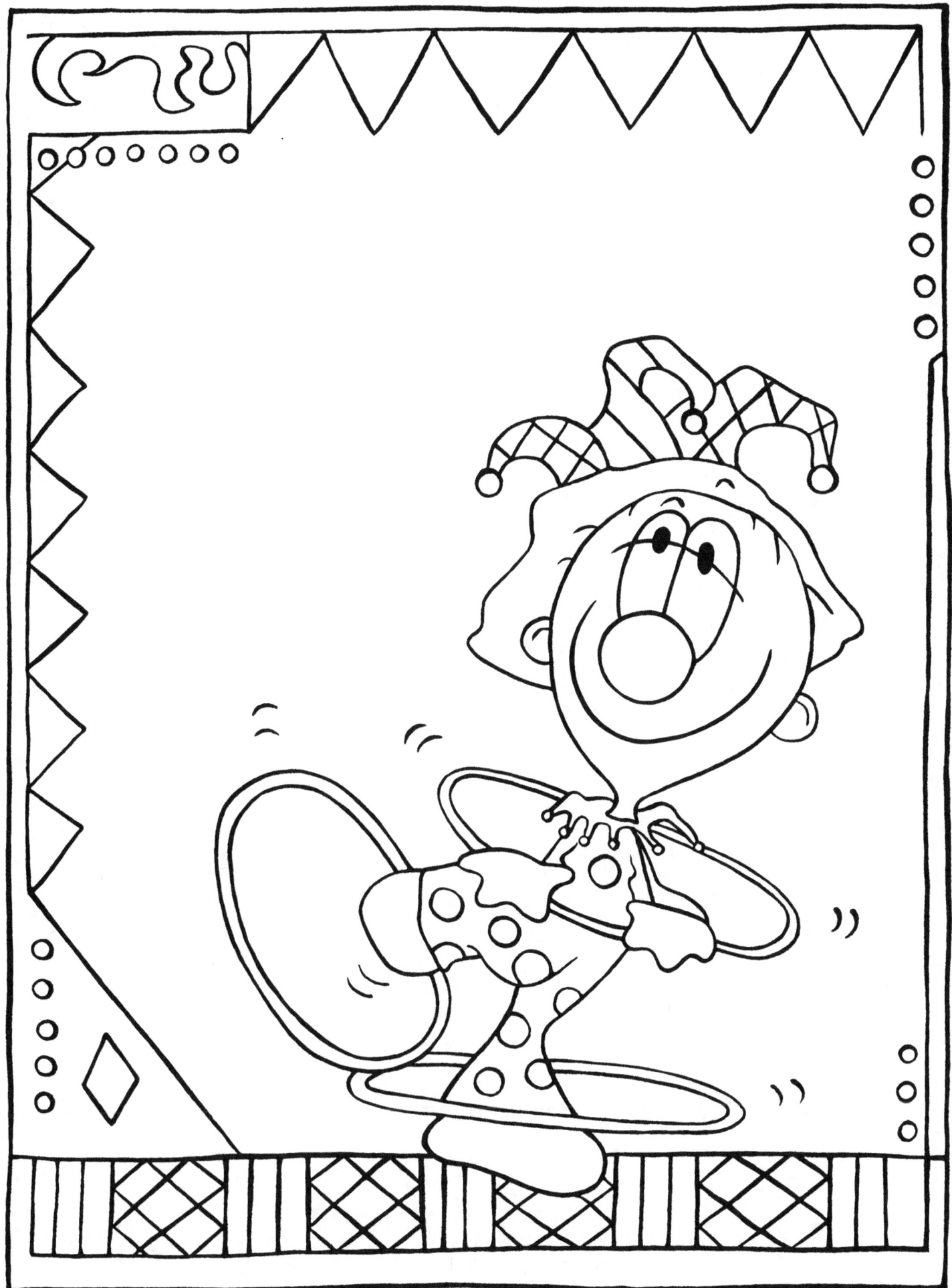

Jester says:
When the only flavors left are banana and licorice—
Learn to *like* banana and licorice!
Things could be a *fompin'* lot worse!

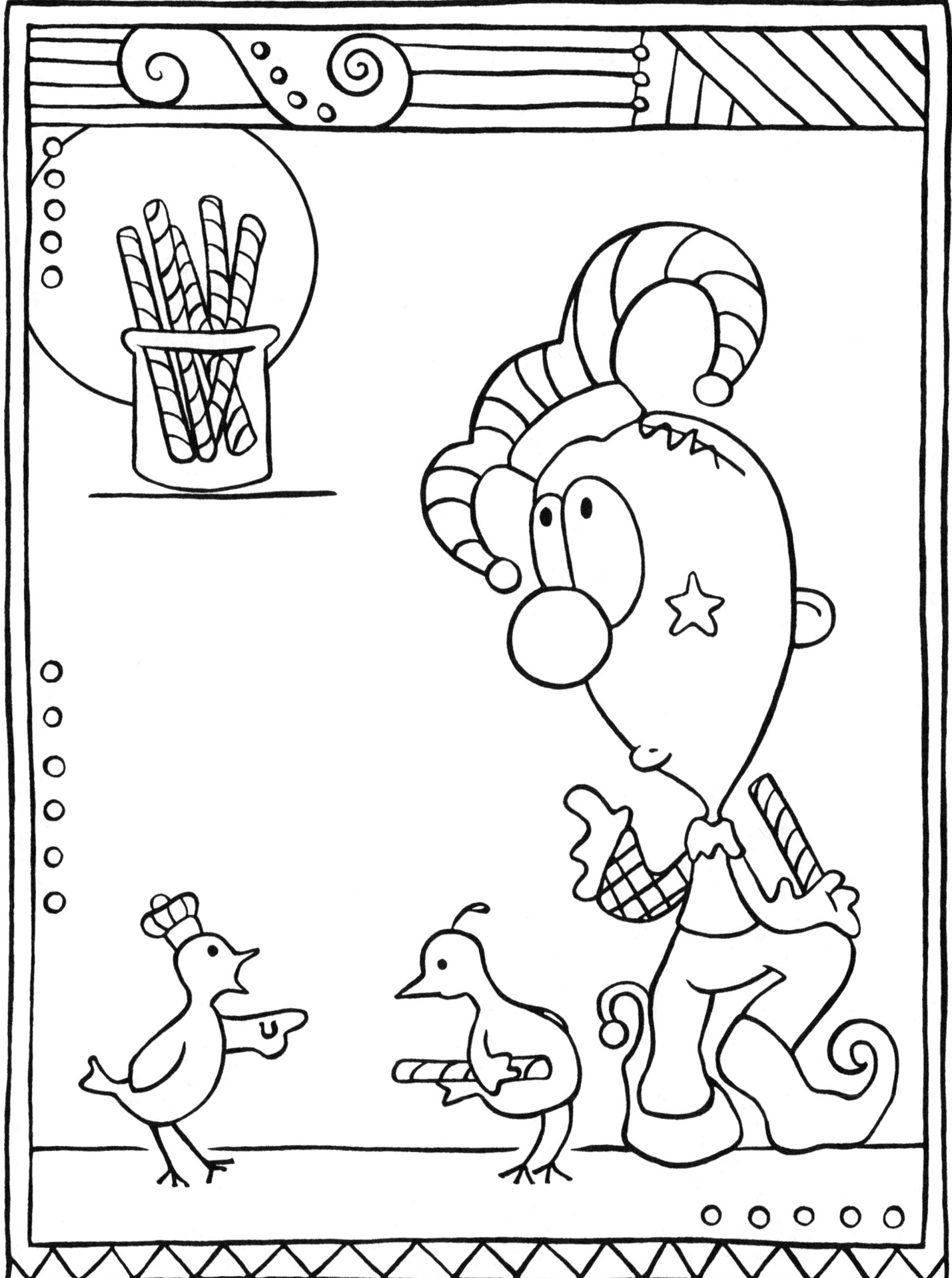

What strangeness
hath this jester wrought?
I don't know what was intended—
But look what she *got!*

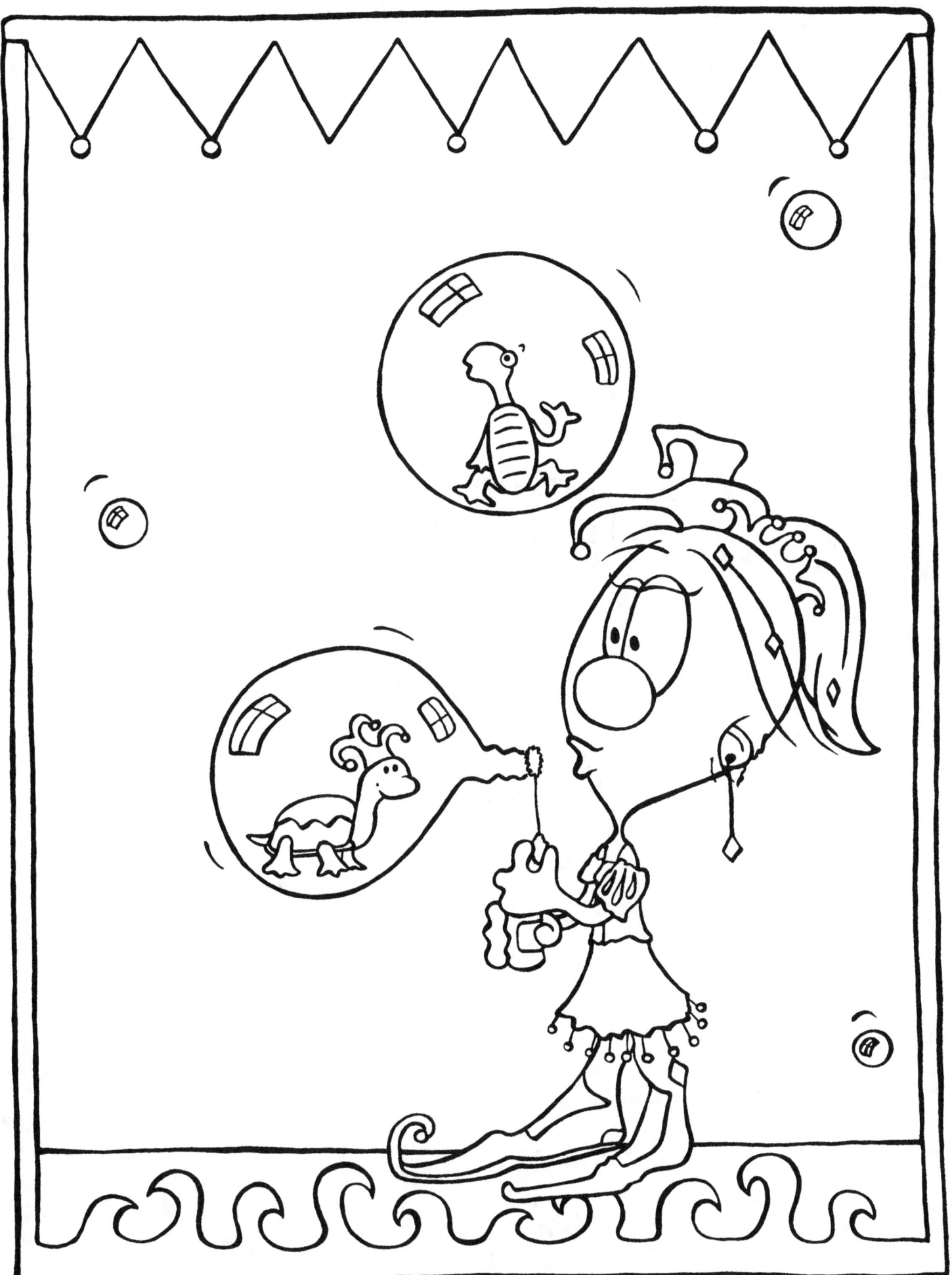

EEEEEEEEEEEEEEEEEEEEEEEEEE
EEEEEEEEEEEEEEEEEEEEEEEEEE
EEEEEEEEEEEEEEEEEEEEEEEEEE
EEEEEEEEEEEEEEEEEEEEEEEEEE
EEEEEEEEEK----------- (GASP) -----------
EEEEEEEEEEEEEEEEEEEEEEEEEE
EEEEEEEEEEEEEEEEEEEEEEEEEE
EEEEEEEEEEEEEEEEEEEEEEEEEE

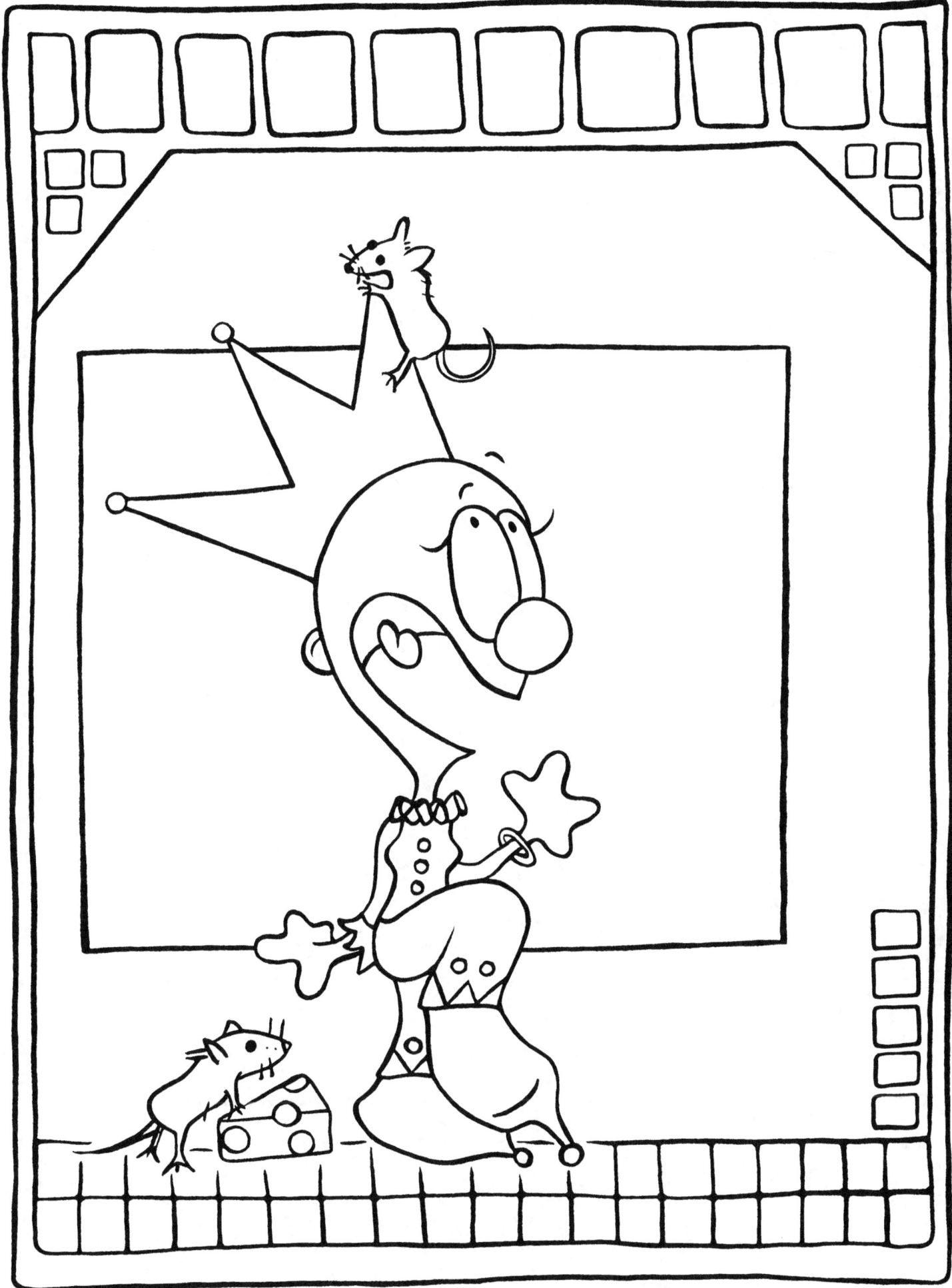

Worst hair day
of my entire friggin' *life!*

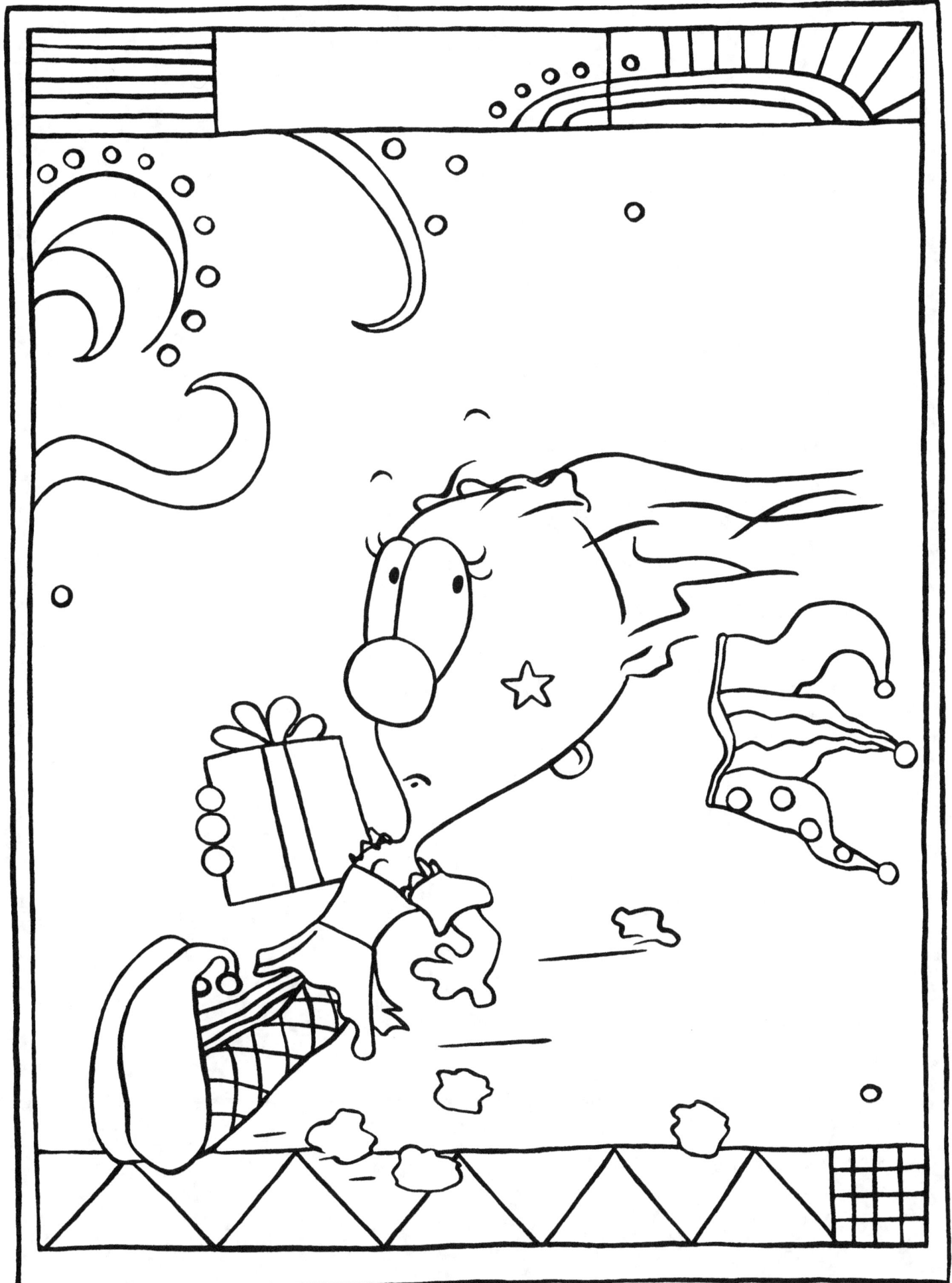

Remember when people used to send those penpal letters in the mail all covered with stickers and pretty stuff?
Let's revisit the practice!
You go first.

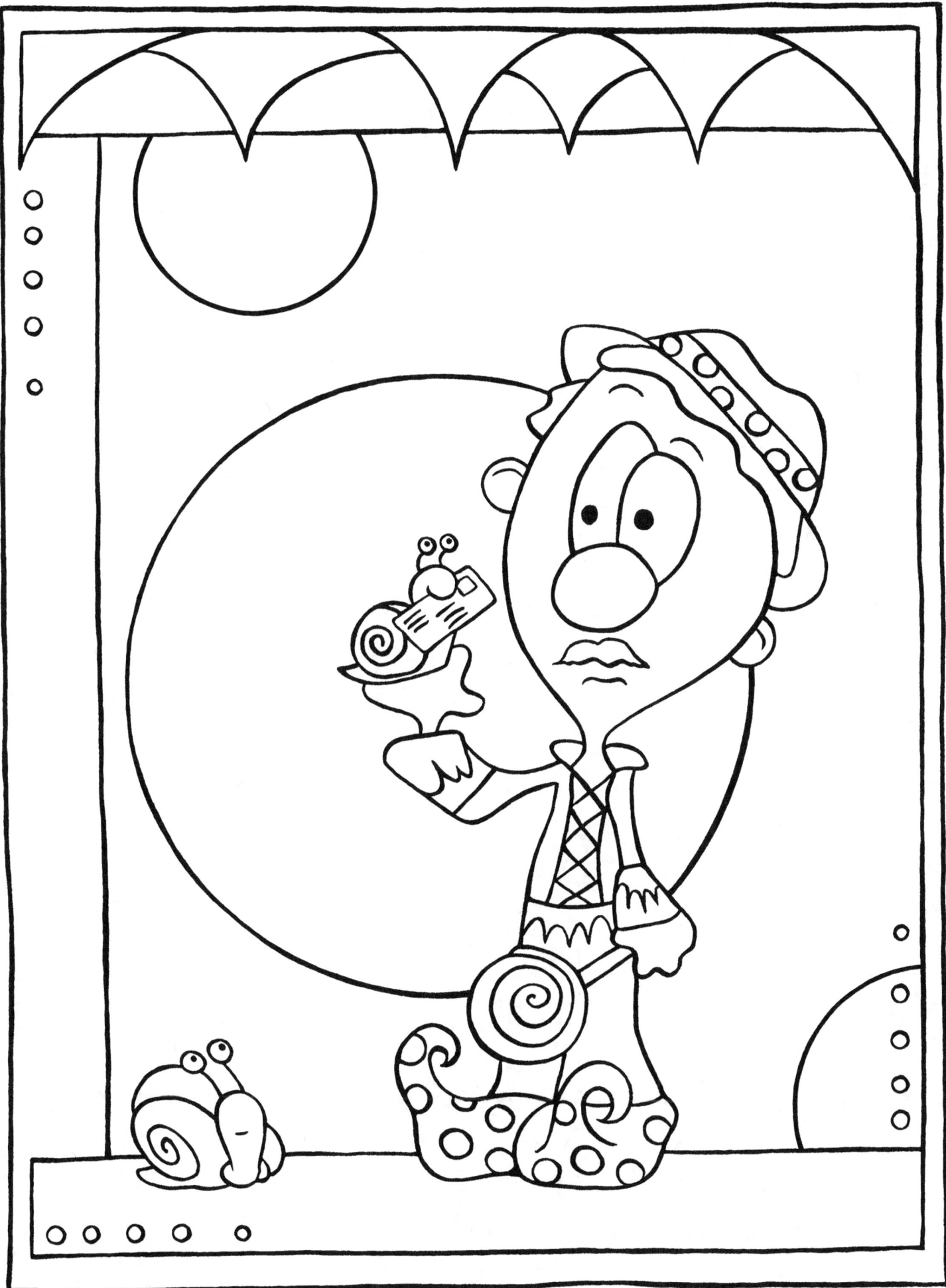

I may play the fool,
but I have the ear of the king.

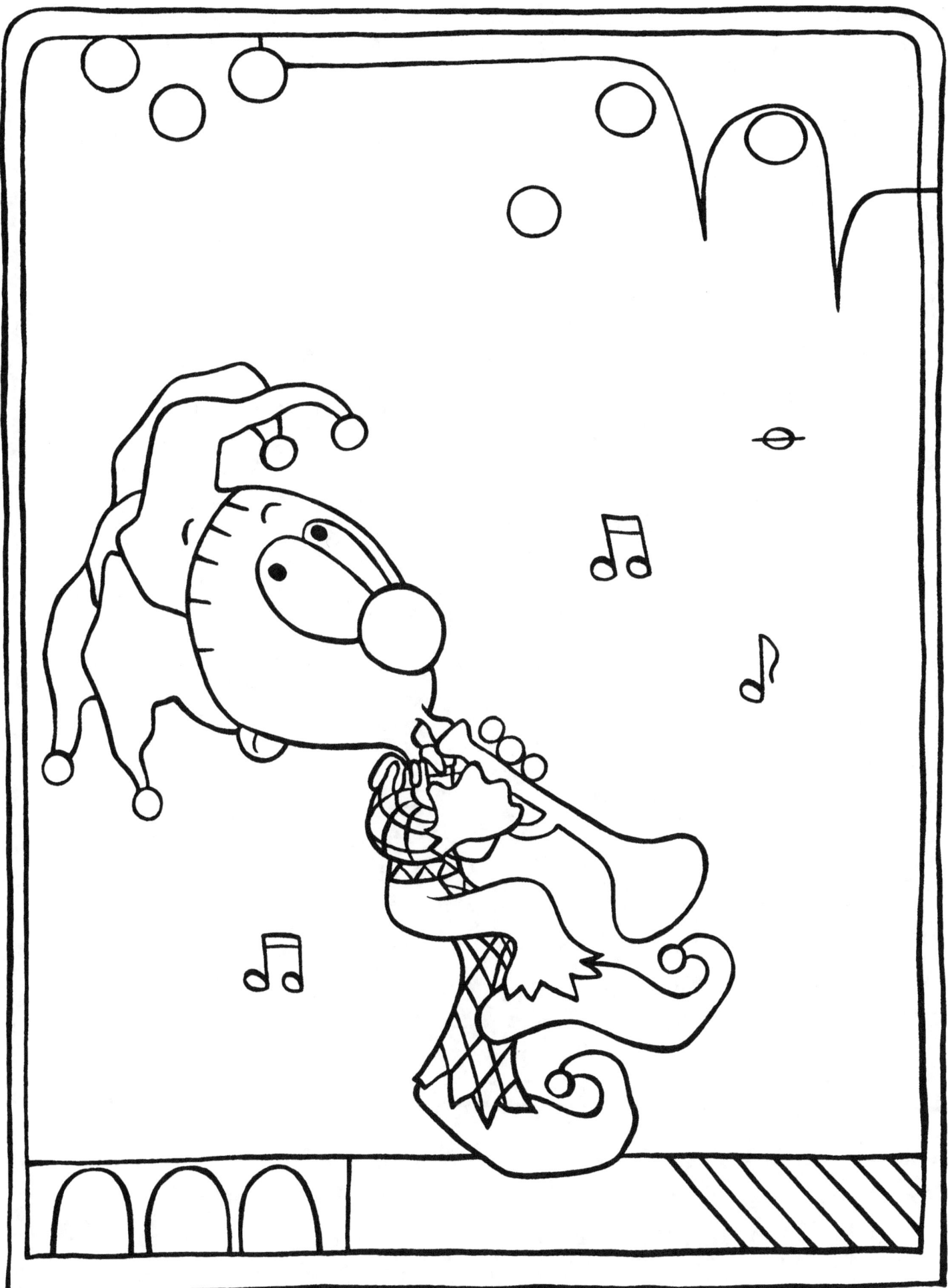

Forget this crapolla!
Did someone say *chocolate?*

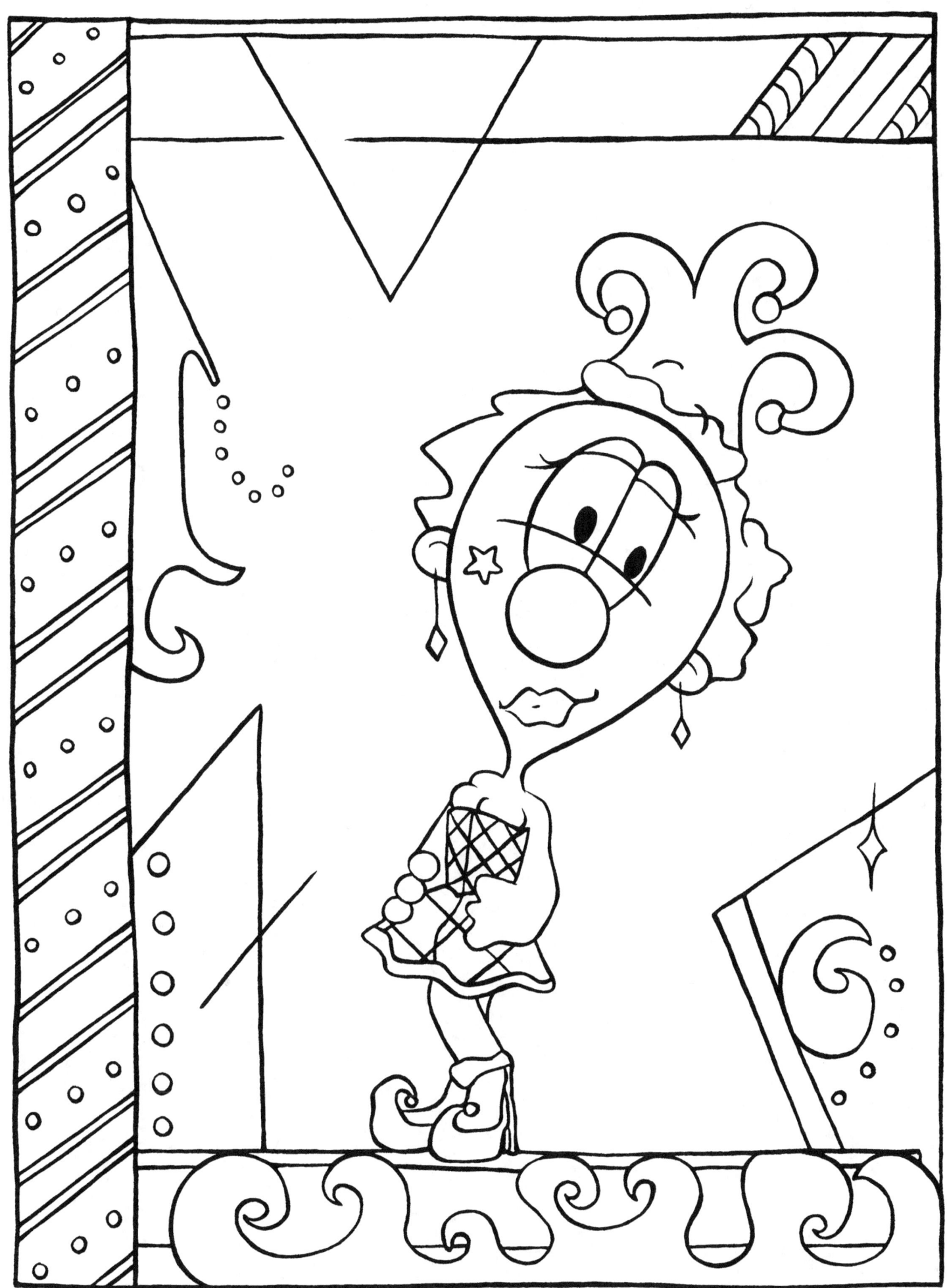

Your name wouldn't be
Glinda the Good Witch, would it?

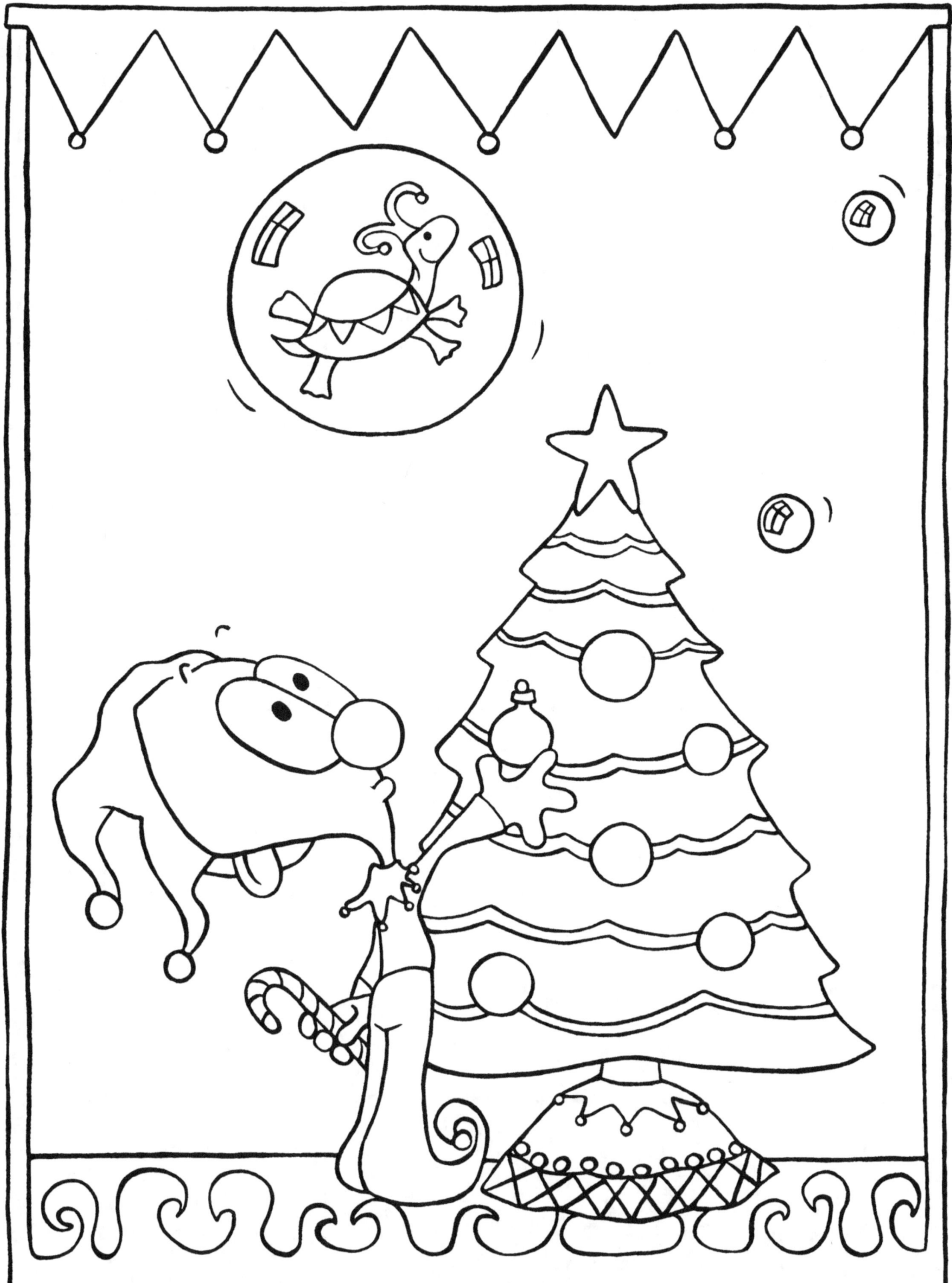

Caesar had his cabbages;
Knights in armour have their jousts—
Me? I'll hang out with ladybugs;
They fly happy 'round the house.

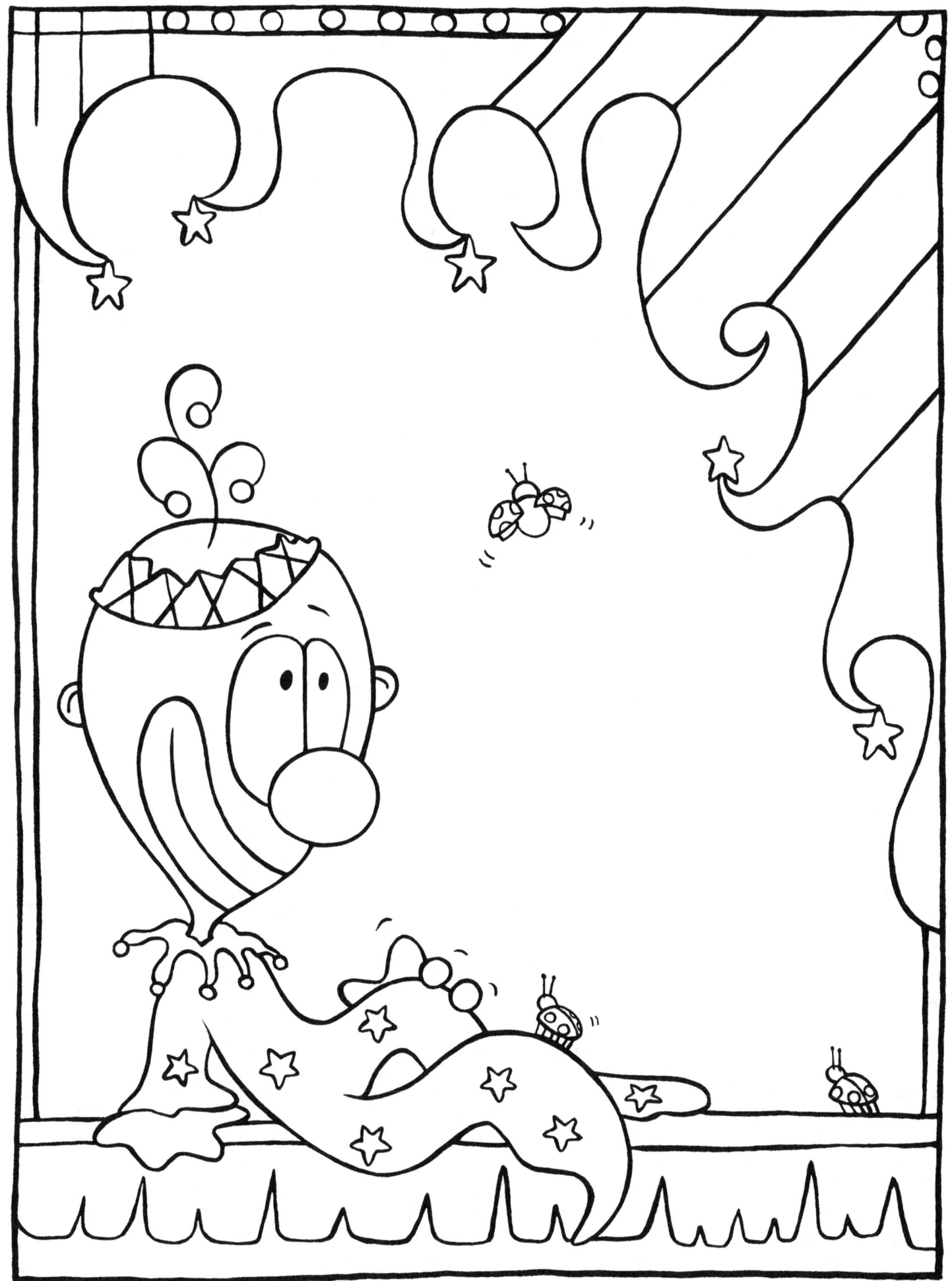

SONNET TO A SNAIL

Here's to all our slimy friends—
I don't know where they're going,
But I know where they've been!

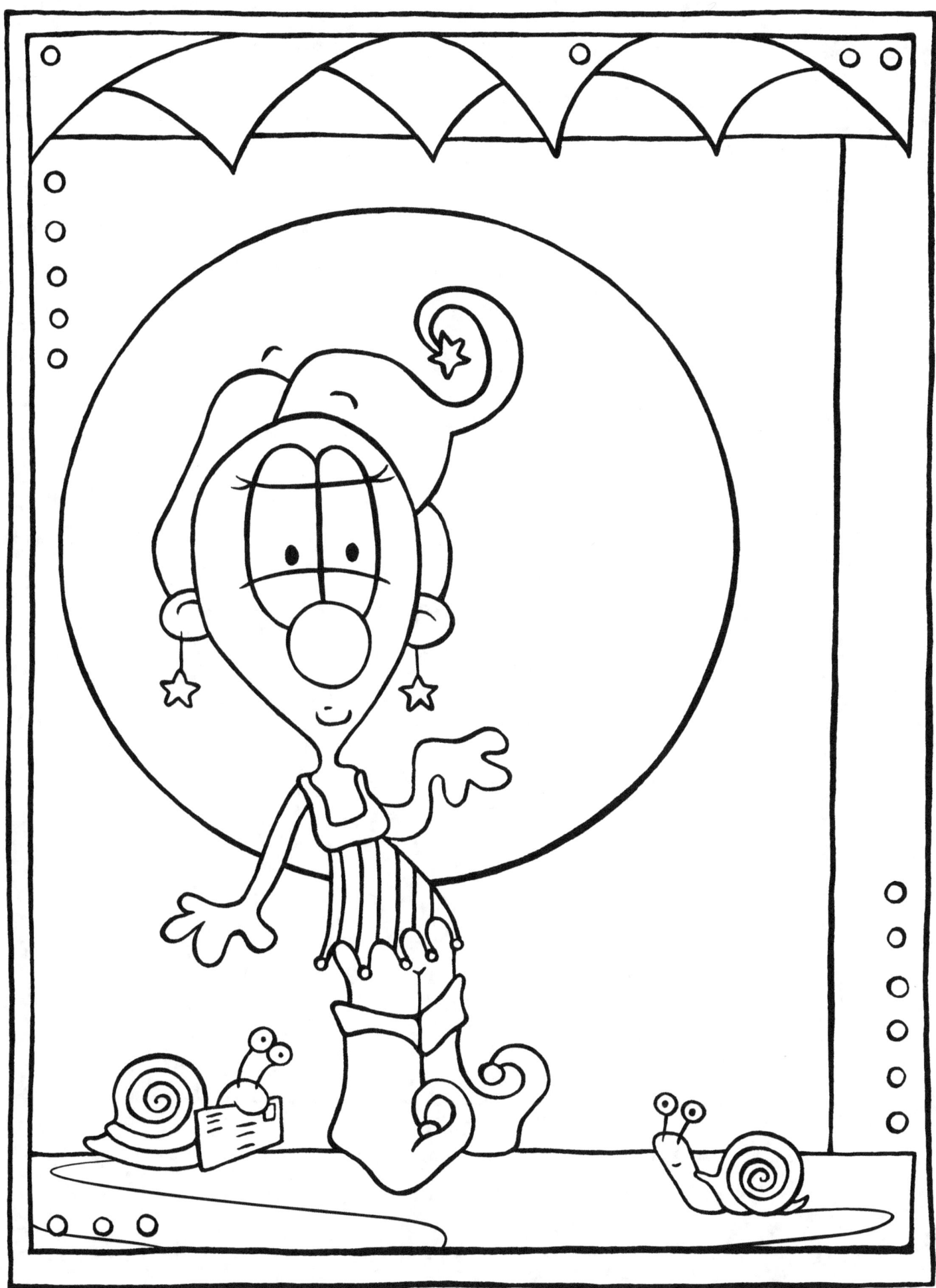

Oh, you laughable launching leapers;
you've got acrobatic skills and giant peepers.

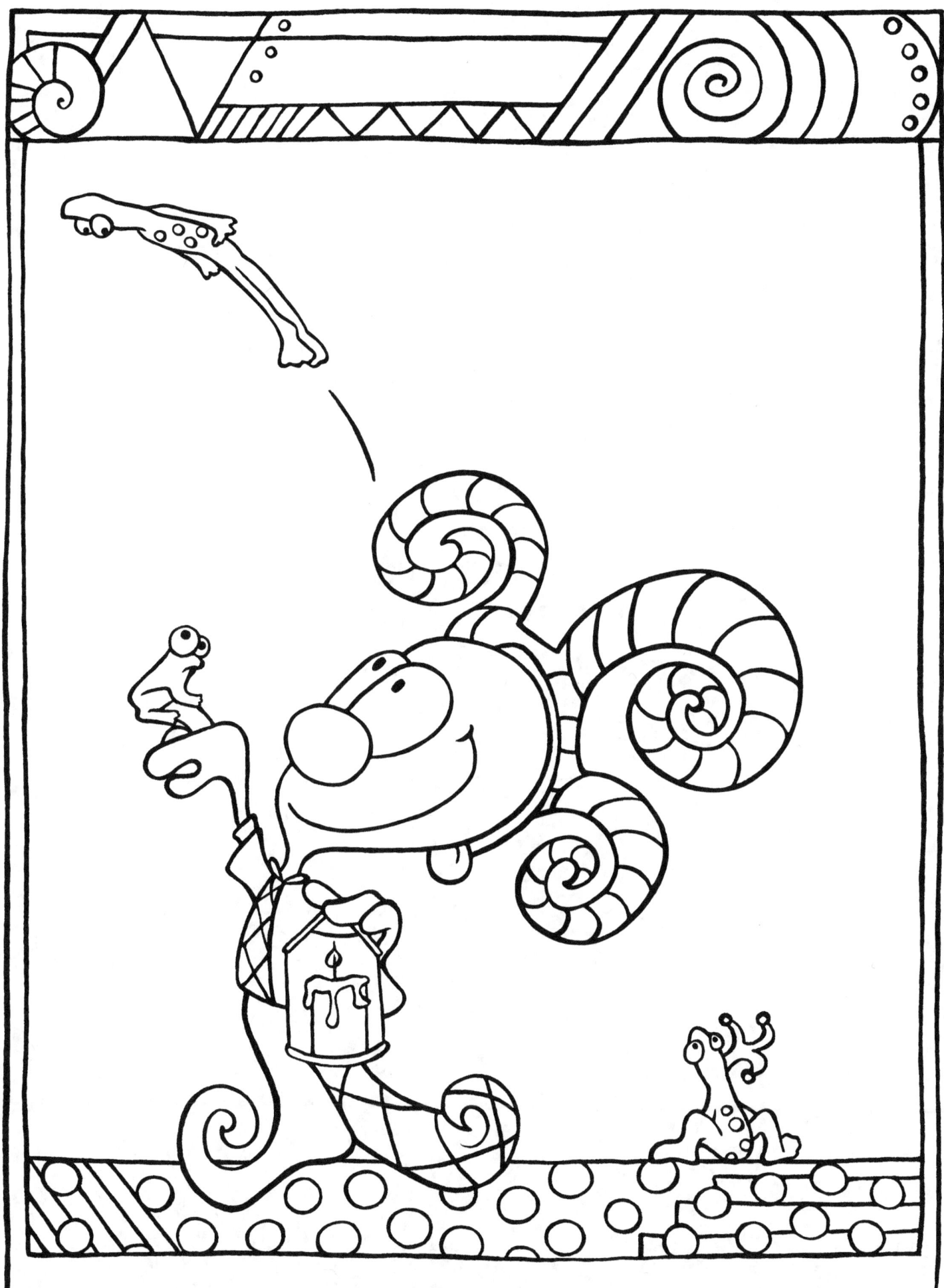

WHAT'S IN THE BOX? WHAT?
WHAT? WHAT? WHAT?!!!
I got a rubber chicken once.
It was the *best*.

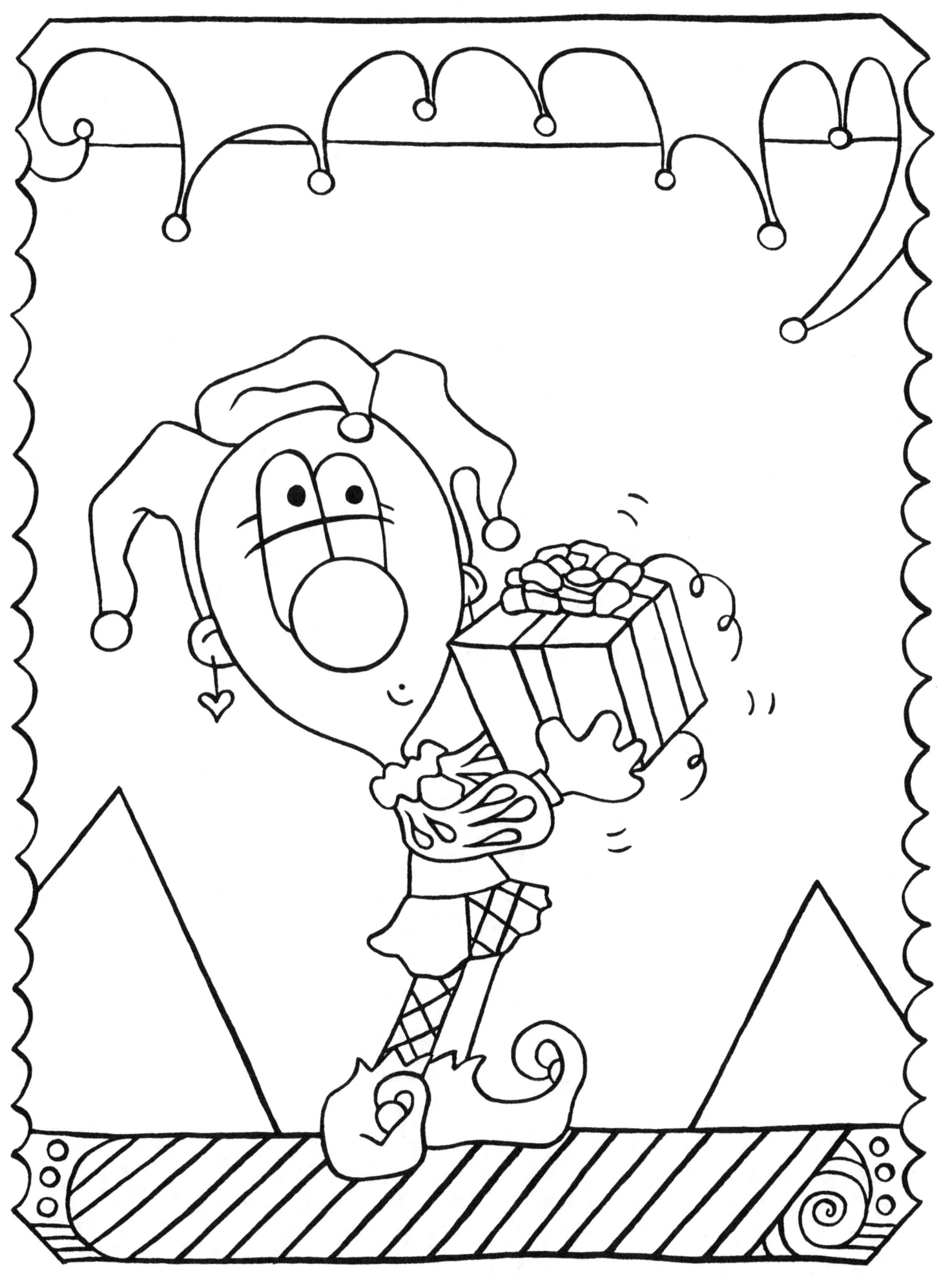

Perfect as punch at a party.
But then, when am I not?

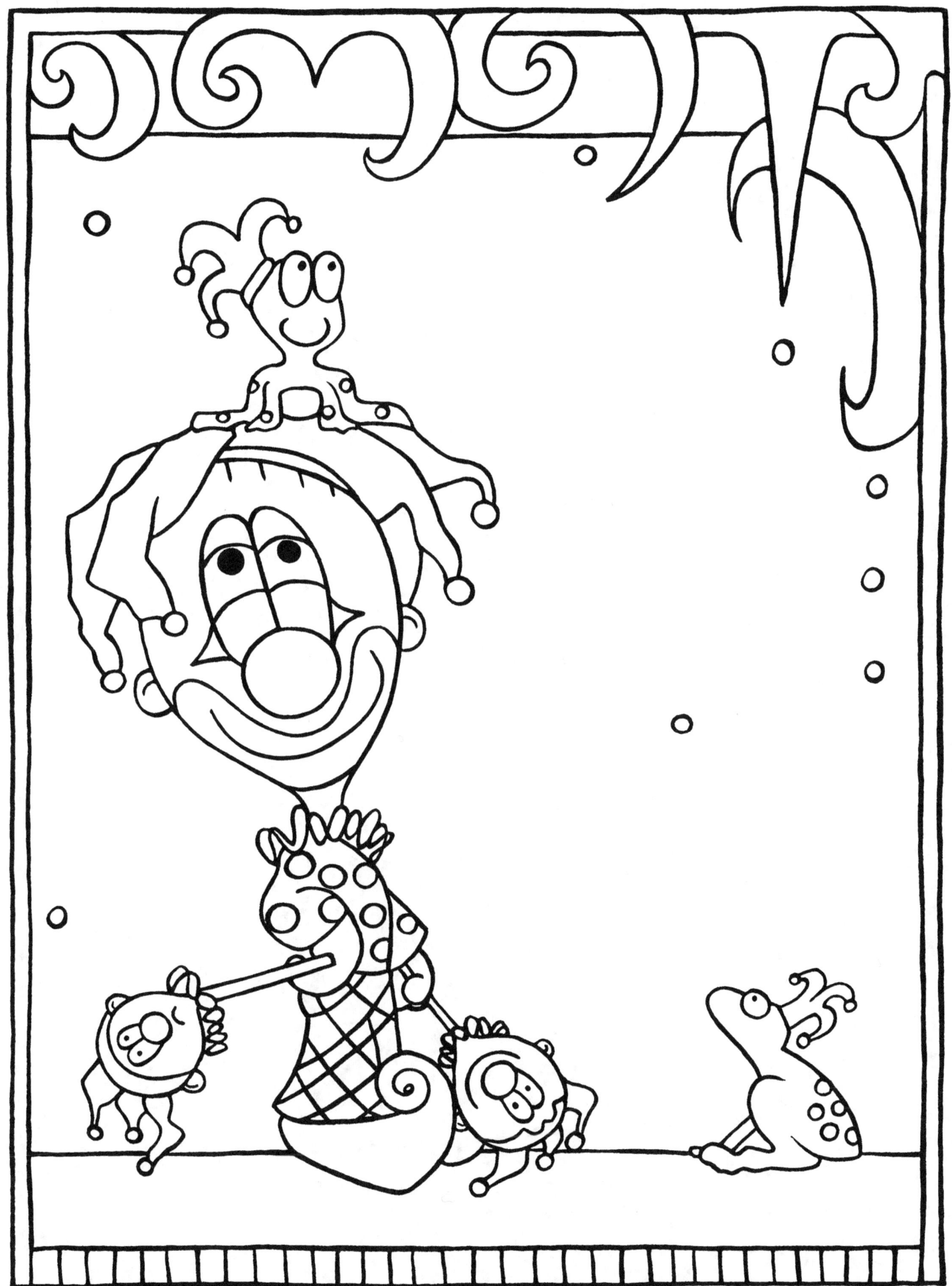

If all the toads were turned to princes,
who would catch the flies?

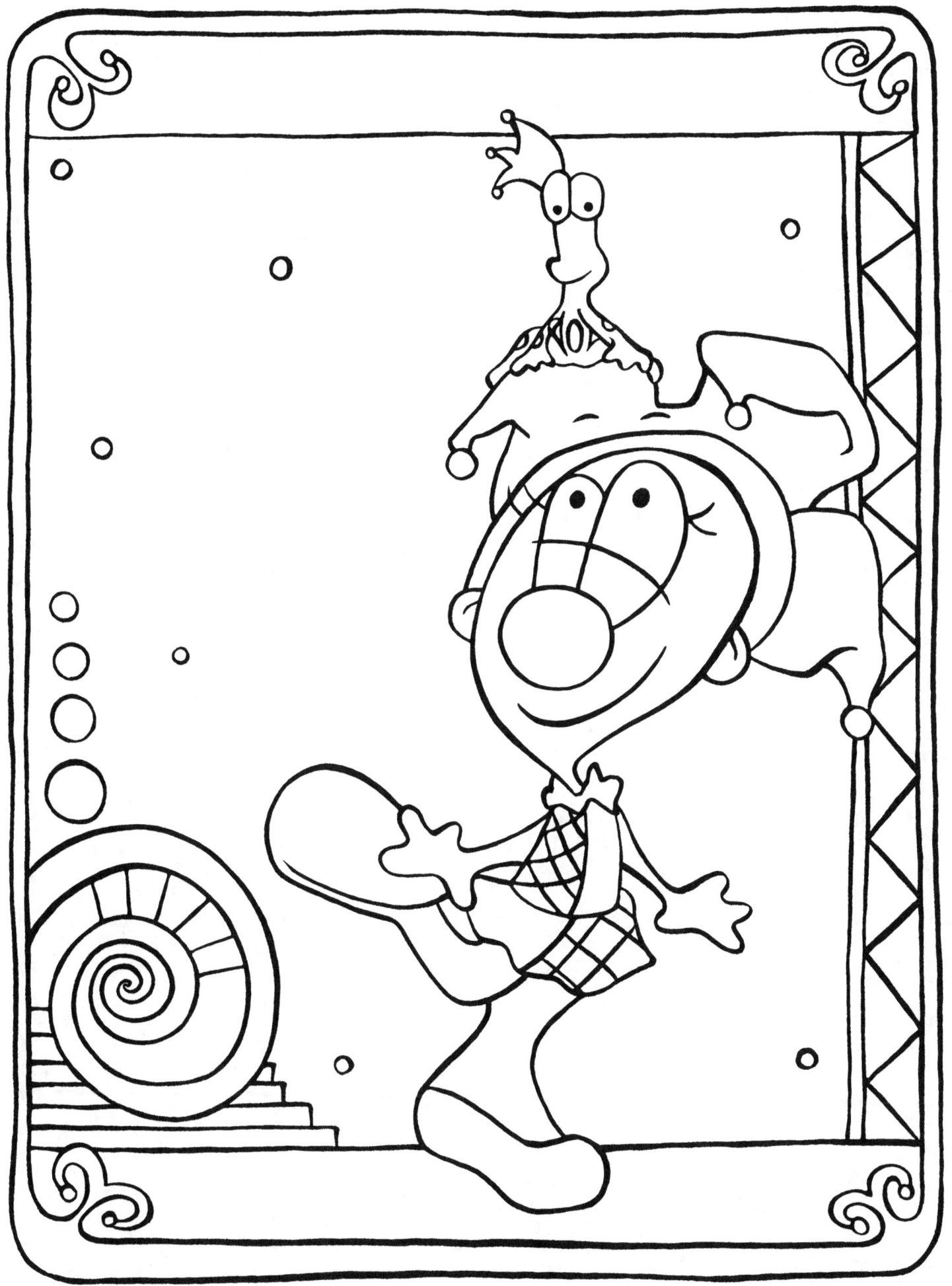

I don't follow trends—
I *make* them.

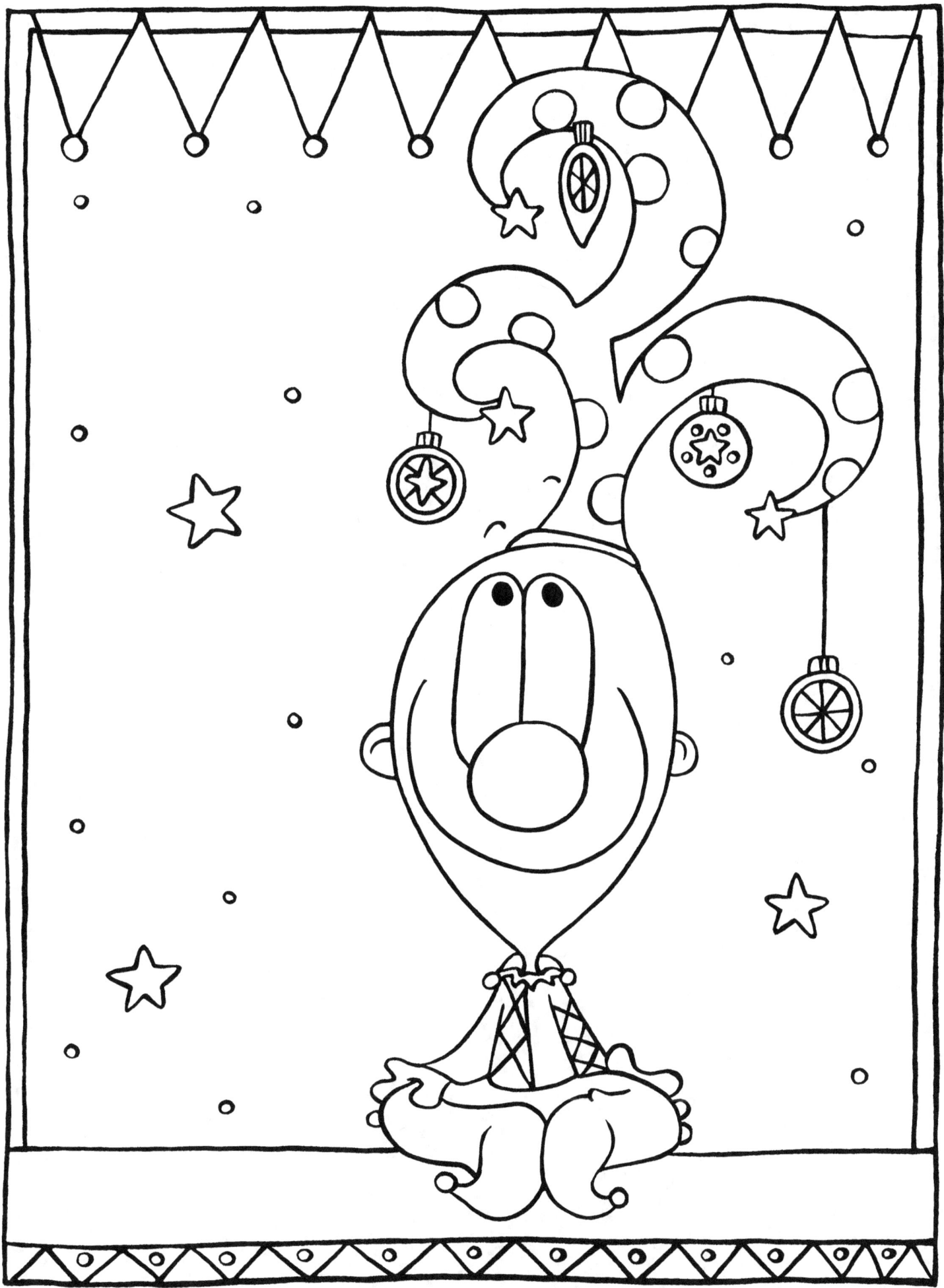

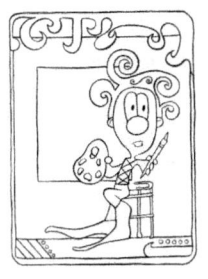 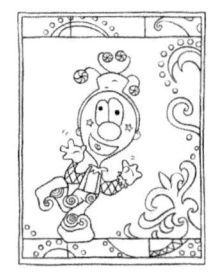 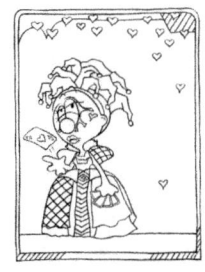 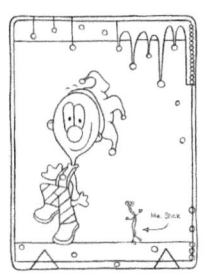 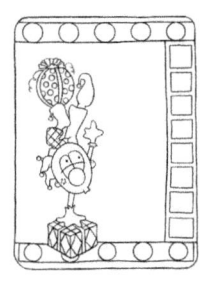 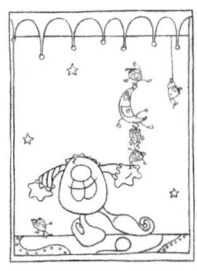
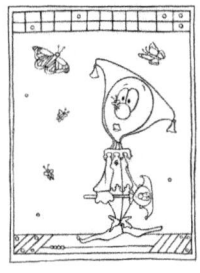 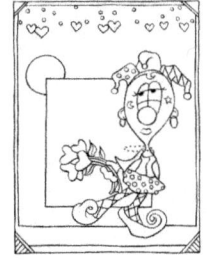 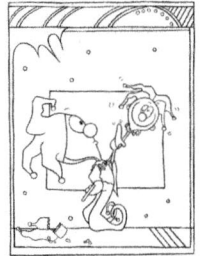 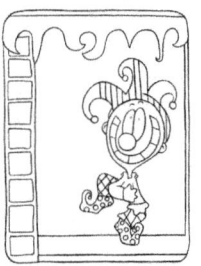 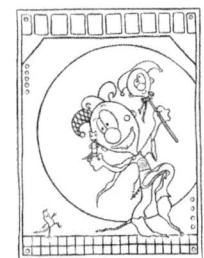 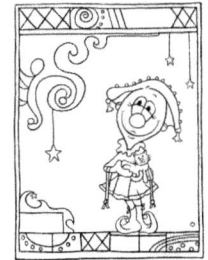

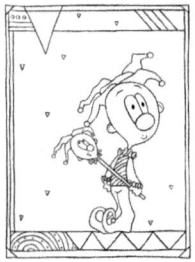 # THE END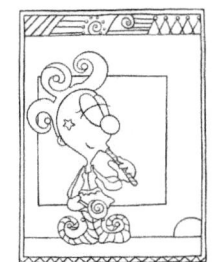

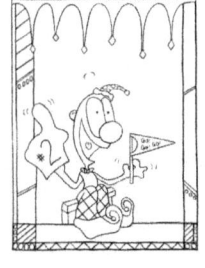 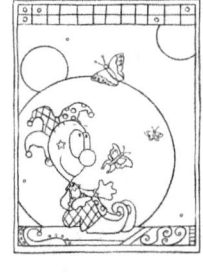 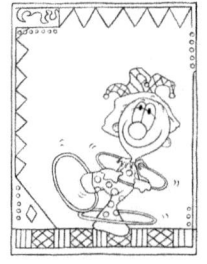 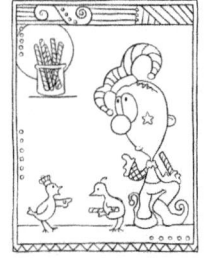 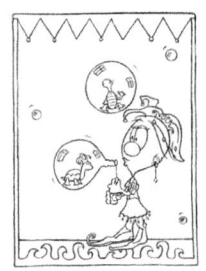 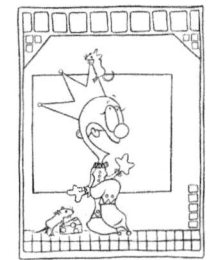
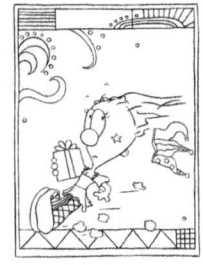 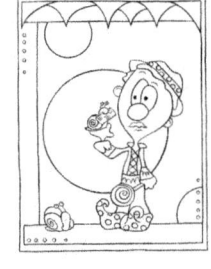 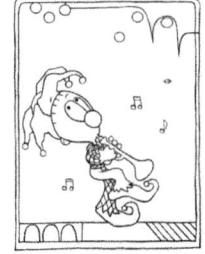 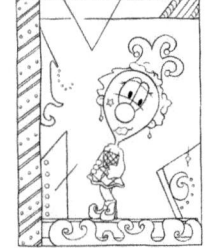 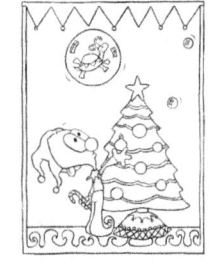 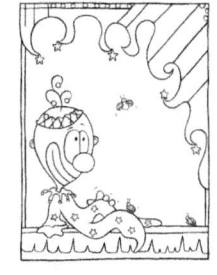
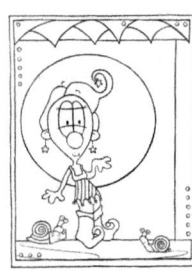 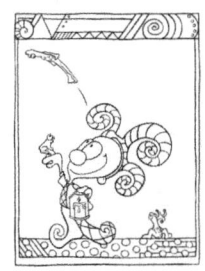 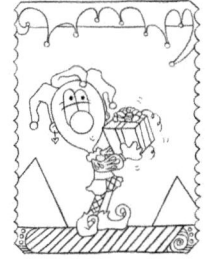 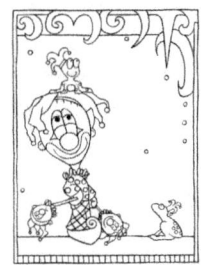 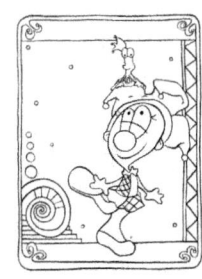 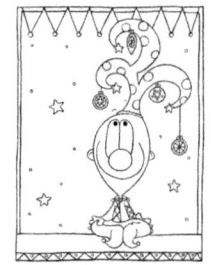

www.ingramcontent.com/pod-product-compliance
Lightning Source LLC
Chambersburg PA
CBHW062336220526
45469CB00008B/2740